顾希佳　编著
周远梅　译
常新萍　英文审校

中國經典文化故事系列

Chinese Classic Cultural Stories Series

中国传说故事

Stories of Chinese Legends

牛郎织女

The Oxherd and the Weaving Maiden

廣東省出版集團

廣東教育出版社

图书在版编目(CIP)数据

牛郎织女／顾希佳编著；周远梅译．—广州：广东教育出版社，2006.9
（中国经典文化故事系列）
ISBN 7-5406-6432-0

Ⅰ．牛…　Ⅱ．①顾…②周…　Ⅲ．①英语—汉语—对照读物②民间故事—中国　Ⅳ．H319.4：I

中国版本图书馆 CIP 数据核字（2006）第 106469 号

广　东　省　出　版　集　团
广 东 教 育 出 版 社 出 版 发 行
（广州市环市东路 472 号 12-15 楼）
邮政编码：510075
网址：http://www.gjs.cn
广东新华发行集团股份有限公司经销
佛山市浩文彩色印刷有限公司印刷
（南海区狮山科技工业园 A 区）
850 毫米 × 1168 毫米　32 开本　3.625 印张　100 000 字
2006 年 9 月第 1 版　2006 年 9 月第 1 次印刷
ISBN 7-5406-6432-0/H · 119
定价：8.40 元
质量监督电话：020-87613102　购书咨询电话：020-34120440

CONTENTS 目录

夏天的夜晚，一大群孩子聚在庭院里，大家都喜欢仰起头来望天空，那儿繁星闪烁。有一条白茫茫的银河，横穿南北，苍苍茫茫，气势磅礴。银河的东边，有一颗发着青色光辉的星星，边上还紧挨着四颗小星，活像是一台织布机，大伙儿都叫它织女星。银河的西边呢，有一颗亮闪闪的星星和织女星遥遥相对，在它的一前一后又有两颗小星，看起来就像一个人挑着一副担子似的，大伙儿都叫它牵牛星。

On summer nights, a throng of kids are gathering together in the courtyard, looking up to the starry sky where the the Milky Way[1] extends from the north to the south, boundless and overwhelming. To its east, a blue blazed star, nestled by four tiny ones, looks just like a loom. Thus Chinese people call the star Vega the Weaving Maiden (Zhinu). To its west, another brilliant star gazing into the distance, with two tiny ones at its back and front, looks like a man carrying two children in baskets strung from a shoulder pole. Thus Chinese people call the star Altair Oxherd (Niulang).

每当这个时候，老人一边指点着天上的牵牛星和织女星，一边就会讲述起《牛郎织女》的故事来。这个动听的故事起码讲了二千多年啦，世世代代传下来，大伙儿都朝那故事里添加点东西进去，于是故事就变得越来越好听，越来越好听，让人百听不厌。

1. In Chinese, the Milky Way is called “the Silver Way”.

Usually at this moment, the grannies will point out into the sky and begin to tell the story of *Niulang and Zhinu*. This story has been told for more than 2,000 years, from generations to generations. Every time when it is told, people would like to add something new to it, making it more attractive to the ears. That is why people are never tired of it no matter how many times they have heard of it.

一、兄弟分家

1. The Division of the Family

从前，山里有一户人家，爹娘死得早，只剩下两兄弟。哥哥已经成了家，有了老婆。弟弟还没成亲，一家三口人，靠种地过日子。

Once upon a time, in the mountains, there lived a family with only two brothers whose parents died when they were young. The elder brother got married while the younger brother remained single all the time. Three of them lived together, on planting.

弟弟不会花言巧语，老实巴交的，只知道埋头干活，别的啥也不琢磨，别人都叫他“傻蛋”。傻蛋干活勤快，所以他的饭量也就特别大，一个顶俩。他嫂子总是嫌他吃得多，心疼粮食，就一天到晚扁着嘴骂他“傻吃”。

The younger brother was a man of few words. He knew nothing but to work hard, thus the nickname “Fool”. Fool always kept his hands full, so he had grand appetite for food. Sometimes he ate twice as much as an ordinary man. His sister-in-law strongly disliked this, thinking that it was a great waste of food. So she cursed him “Fool” every day from morning till night.

弟弟听老人说，山里躺着一头老黄牛，不吃不喝，躺了好多年啦，怪可怜的。他就决心要进山去把老牛拉回来耕田。他把这事跟哥哥一说，哥哥正想要添一头牛呢。就一口答应了，让他早去早回。

The younger brother had heard old villagers say that there was a yellow ox that had been lying in the mountains without food and drink for many years. He felt greatly pitiful for him, so he determined to go into the mountains and take the ox back home to plough for him. When he talked it over with his elder brother, the elder brother didn't oppose him, since this was exactly what he was considering to have another ox in the family. So the elder brother let him go and told him to come back home as early as possible.

那天，弟弟一个人背了点干粮，就进了大山，翻过九十九道岭，淌过九十九道涧，果然看见那儿有一头瘦骨嶙峋的老黄牛，在一块大平石上躺着呢。他走过去趴下向老牛磕了个头，喊一声："牛大伯，跟我回家去吧，我来养你。"

On that very day, the younger brother went into the mountains with the solid food alone. After he had tramped over many hills and dales, as expected, he saw a skinny ox lying on a big flat stone. He slowly approached the ox, stooped and made a bow before him, saying, “Uncle Ox, come back home with me! I will feed you.”

老黄牛睁开眼来，看了看他，闷声不响，又懒洋洋地把眼睛闭上了。弟弟看着老牛没精打采的样子，好可怜，心里想：它一定是饿了吧。就赶紧去拔草。

The old yellow ox opened his eyes, looked at him dumbly and closed his eyes again languidly. When the younger brother saw that the yellow ox was listless, a sense of sympathy suddenly burst out of his heart. “He must be quite hungry,” he thought. Then he rushed to pull grass for the ox.

说来也怪，弟弟拔来的草，老牛总是会大口大口地吃下去。弟弟拔多少，老牛吃多少，弟弟拔了一捆又一捆，老牛张开嘴巴，一会儿工夫就吃完了，总是供不上，这下可把弟弟给累坏了。不过弟弟心里却挺高兴的，既然老牛爱吃，就多拔些吧，拔草也累不着，就一个劲地去拔草。

The younger brother was surprised to see that, the yellow ox almost wolfed down all the grass that he had pulled for him. No matter how much grass the younger brother gave to him, the yellow ox swallowed it up at a gulp. One pile of grass after another, the old ox opened his mouth and ate them all up. The younger brother was exhausted yet he was very happy. “Now that the ox likes eating, I will pull more. I will never be hurt by pulling grass," he thought. Then he began to pull more grass with all his strength.

一连喂了三天，老黄牛终于吃饱了，抬起头来，跟他说了一番知心话："小弟弟，多谢你来喂我，你知道吗？我原先是住在天上的。当初盘古开天辟地的时候，地上没有五谷，全靠着我去偷来了天仓里的五谷种，撒了下来，地上的百姓才能够种上粮食。可这事却让玉皇大帝发觉了，他大发脾气，一脚把我踢下天庭。结果我就摔坏了腿，躺在这儿这么多年了，谁也不来喂我。你是个好孩子，自己还饿着肚子呢。却一连喂了我三天，从此以后，我们就是好朋友了，你说吧，我该怎么谢谢你？"

For the next three days it was like this. Eventually the yellow ox became full. Slowly he raised his head, and started to pour his heart to the younger brother, "Thank you for feeding me, Little Brother. You know, I used to live in the Heaven. At the beginning of the Opening of the Earth, there was no corn growing in the fields. It was I who stole the seeds of the five types of corn from the Barn of Heaven and scattered them down to the Earth so that people could plant grains on the ground. This irritated the Jade Emperor in the Heaven a lot. Knowing this, he flew into a rage, and kicked me out of the Heaven. My legs were broken then. I have been lying here for many years. No one came to feed me except you. Good Boy! If it had not been for you, I would still have been starving. Now that you have fed me for three days, we have become good pals. How should I thank you? Just tell me."

弟弟说："牛大伯，你跟我回家吧，我天天拔草来喂你。"

The younger brother said, "Uncle Ox, come back home with me. I assure you that I will feed you grass every day."

"好哇！不过眼下还不行，我的伤还没养好呢，得用百花露水涂洗一百天才会好。"

"Good! But not now. My wounds have not been completely healed yet. It needs to be wiped and cleansed with the dew from a hundred flowers for a hundred days."

弟弟一口答应，也就不急着下山了。他饿了采些野果子吃，渴了就喝泉水，夜里抱着老黄牛睡觉，每天清晨起来，就去采百花，用花朵上的露水给老黄牛洗伤。整整忙了一百天，果然把老黄牛的伤给养好啦。老黄牛站起身，高高兴兴地跟着他回家了。

The younger brother replied to him with a glad "Yes". He was not in a hurry to go out of the mountains. When he was hungry, he picked up some wild fruits to stuff his stomach; when he was thirsty, he drank some water from the mountain springs. At nights, he embraced the ox and slept together with him. Every morning he got up at dawn to collect the flowers, and with the dews from the flowers he cleansed the wounds

of the yellow ox. This continued for a hundred days. Finally the wounds of the yellow ox were healed, and then he rose up on his feet, following the younger brother home happily.

哥哥嫂嫂见他居然能牵回一头牛来，倒也蛮高兴，就没有骂他。从此以后，放牛的事全都交给了他。弟弟一门心思放牛，待老黄牛就像是自己的亲人一样，白天和老牛一起上山，到了夜里，他把牛棚垫得干干的，自己也睡在牛棚里。一有闲空，就给老牛梳毛，给老牛割草，把老牛侍候得膘满肉肥，毛色闪闪发亮，溜光溜光的，谁见了都要夸上几句。村里人从此都把他叫做"牛郎"。

It was a great surprise for the elder brother and sister-in-law to see the younger brother back home with an ox. They did not scold him. On the contrary, they were very happy. Ever since, the job of ox-herding was on him. The only thing that the younger brother dwelt on every day was to herd the ox. He treated the ox as his own family. In the daytime he went to the mountain with the ox while at night he filled up the ox-shed and slept in it with the ox. Once he had time, he combed the hair for the ox, and cut grass to feed it. The ox was so well-fed and soon it became fat and fleshy with shining and smooth hair. Everyone who saw the ox would like to praise the oxherd. Soon the younger brother got another nickname "Oxherd" (Niulang).

嫂子小心眼，单等牛郎出门干活去了，她就在家里做烙饼，下饺子，夫妻两人吃香的喝辣的；等牛郎一回家，却喝的是烂菜汤，吃的是糠窝头，天天都是这样。

The sister-in-law was snorty and narrow-minded. She often prepared the flapjack and dumplings when Niulang was working away from home. She and her husband ate the fine food while she had Niulang eat the leftovers and the roughage. Every day it was like this.

这天，牛郎耕地耕到前半晌，老黄牛开口说话了："牛郎，你嫂子正在包饺子呢，你不回家吃好的去？"

One day, amidst the ploughing, the yellow ox started to speak, "Niulang, your sister-in-law is preparing dumplings. Why don't you go back and eat?"

"嘿，我这么早就回去，人家会骂的。"

"No! If I go back so early, I will be blamed," said Niulang.

"哎，你想回就回吧，到家正好饺子也熟了，怕啥？"

"Why! If you'd like to go back, you can. When you arrive at home, it is the right time to eat the dumplings. What are you afraid of ?"

"那我怎么回？"

"How can I do this?" Niulang asked.

牛郎一向老实，他觉得没有什么理由，总不能提前收工回家的吧。

Niulang was honest in nature. He thought it was not good to be home ahead of time if no sound excuses could be offered.

老牛眨巴着眼睛，给他出了个主意："这还不好办？南边地头有块大石头，咱们耕地耕到那里，一使劲把铧子给砸坏了，就一块儿回去吧。"

Then the yellow ox blinked his eyes, and thought up a good idea, " That's easy! In the south field, there will be a big stone. When we arrive there, we hit the stone with the plough-share. Then we can go home."

说着说着，他们已经耕到那块大石头跟前了，老牛猛地朝前一冲，牛郎心领神会，赶紧朝前一跟，再往后一拽，只听得"嘣"的一声，就把铧子给砸坏了。好哇！牛郎闷声不响，赶着牛回家。

Right at that moment, they arrived at the big stone. The yellow ox rushed forward, Niulang followed him closely, and pulled back. The plough-share broke with a big crash. My Goodness! Niulang headed for home quietly with the ox.

到家里，果然没错，他嫂子正在左一碗右一碗地忙着往外捞饺子呢，一抬头，怎么牛郎回来了？倒有点不好意思起来，只好假惺惺地喊他："兄弟，我正想让人去叫你呢。你真有口福，我刚捞出来，你就到了，快去吃吧。"

As they got home, it was true that the sister-in-law was busy spooning out the dumplings, one bowl after another. She raised her head and was surprised to find that Niulang was there! A little bit embarrassed, she pretended to invite him to have the dumplings together, "Brother! I am thinking of having you back home to have lunch. You really have good luck for good food. The moment I spoon the dumplings out, you are here. Do come and eat with us!"

他哥哥却板着脸盘问起来："你怎么这么早就收工了？"

However, his elder brother questioned him with a straightened face, "Why do you knock off so early?"

牛郎红着脸说："不小心，把铧子给砸坏了，没法耕啦。"

"The plough-share was broken out of a sudden. I couldn't plough without it," Niulang replied with a reddened face.

哥哥过去一看，果然是铧子砸坏了，只好闷声不响，坐在一边抽烟。牛郎老实不客气，坐下来饱饱吃了一顿。吃饱了，抹抹嘴，又赶着牛老老实实干活去了。到了地里，老牛说："你说那饺子香不香？我没说错吧？下回等她做了好吃的，我再告诉你。"

The elder brother came up to have a look. The ploughshare was truly broken. He had to sit there silently, smoking. Niulang was basically honest. He just sat down and ate. After eating, he wiped his mouth and drove the ox to the field again. When they came back to the field, the old ox started to speak again, "Don't you think that the dumplings are delicious? Next time if she makes more delicious food, I will tell you again."

第二天，牛郎还是早早地就出门去耕地，快晌午的时候，老牛又提醒他了："牛郎，今天晌午家里人吃包子哩，走吧。"

The next day Niulang went out to plough the field at early hours. When midday came, the old ox reminded him again, "Niulang, today's lunch is *baozi*. Let's go."

"不，今天我不回去了。"

"No! I won't go today."

"怕什么？回去吧。"

"What are you afraid of ? Come on !"

"怎么回？"

"How can I?"

"老办法，北边地头不是还有块大石头吗？咱们耕地耕到那里，把犁也给弄坏了，就一块儿回去吧。”

“The same! There is another big stone in the north field. When we arrive there, we will break the plough. Then we can go home.”

说着说着又到了大石头跟前，老办法，先是老牛朝前一冲，再是牛郎朝前一跟，又往后一拽，只听得“嘭”的一声响，就把犁也给弄坏了。好吧，反正也没法耕地了，牛郎闷声不响，收拾收拾，赶着牛回家。

At that moment, they arrived at the big stone. Like the day before, the old ox struck forth, and Niulang followed then pulled backward. The plough broke with a bang. That’s it! The plough was broken. They had to go back home. Silently Niulang collected the utensils and drove the ox back home.

嫂子一见，牛郎怎么又回来了，他怎么知道我蒸包子了？她憋了一肚子的火，开口就骂：“说好了给你送饭的，你怎么没头没脑地跑回来了？”

Seeing Niulang back home again, the sister-in-law was furious. She thought, “How does he know that I am steaming *baozi*?” She could not contain her anger any more and started to curse him, “I told you that I would have the lunch sent to you. Who asks you to come back so early?”

他哥哥也是满肚子不舒服："怎么这么早就收工？田都犁好了？"

His brother was also very uncomfortable with him, "Why so early? Finished the ploughing yet?"

牛郎哭丧着脸，低着头回答："没犁好，是我不小心把犁给弄坏了。"

Niulang put on a long face with grief. He lowered his head and replied, "Not yet. I have broken the plough out of carelessness."

哥哥过去一看，果然是犁口砸了，顿时暴跳如雷，开口骂起人来："败家货！昨天打坏了铧，今天又打坏了犁，你还过不过日子？"

The elder brother came up and looked at the plough. It was truly broken. All of a sudden he stamped with fury, and shouted abuses, "What a black sheep! Yesterday you broke the share. Today, the plough. Do you still want to live?"

嫂子也在一边煽风点火："跟这种光能吃不能干的大傻蛋在一起过日子，真是倒了八辈子霉！还不如趁早分家。"

The sister-in-law stood by and stirred up the trouble, "It is such a misfortune to live with a fool like you who knows nothing but to eat! Why not divide the family as soon as possible!"

不过骂归骂，这包子不是已经蒸好了吗？满屋子都是香味，瞒也瞒不住。说起来总还是一家人，蒸好了的包子哪能不给他吃？嫂子一边嘟嘟囔囔地数落个不停，一边还是不得不把包子端了出来。牛郎的肚子早就饿得咕咕叫，他一句话也没回，低着头只顾吃包子，吃饱了，抹抹嘴，又闷声不响赶着老牛下地干活去了。

A curse was a curse. But the *baozi* was ready on the stove, filling the whole room with the aroma that nobody could resist. After all, they still belonged to one family. The sister-in-law had to take out the *baozi*, but in her mouth she did not stop grumbling. Niulang had been hungry for a long time. He lowered his head and started to eat the *baozi* without uttering a single word at all. After he was full, he wiped his mouth, with the same silent manner, he returned to the field with the ox.

就这样，全靠着老牛通风报信，家里的事情一样也瞒不过他牛郎。今天烙了几张饼，牛郎赶上了；明天炸了几块油糕，牛郎又赶上了，从来不会落空。他嫂子可气坏了，天天指着鼻子骂牛郎，牛郎却从来也不跟嫂子顶嘴，只顾吃饱了干活。

With the ox's timely notifications, Niulang could know exactly what was happening in his house. For instance, how many battercakes were baked today, then Niulang could catch the chance and ate them. And tomorrow how many pancakes would be fried, and Niulang could catch the chance again. It never failed. His sister-in-law was greatly annoyed at this, condemning him every day. But Niulang never talked her back. He just went to field ploughing after he had had enough.

嫂子一个人静下心来，总是在想，牛郎年纪也不小了，按照祖上传来的老规矩，往后有妻没妻总得分给他一半家产的吧。说起来，这份家产还不是全靠我们夫妻俩勤勤恳恳挣下来的，凭什么要分给他一半？哼！想着就浑身不舒服。倒不如来个斩草除根，一不做二不休，把牛郎害死拉倒。

While alone, the sister-in-law calculated, "Niulang is not young any more. According to the local custom, he should get half of the properties from this family no matter whether he is married or not. But almost all of the properties are earned by us two. How could it be that he got half ?" Whenever she thought about this, she felt greatly depressed, "It would be better to cut the seedlings and dig out the roots. As well be hanged for a sheep as for a lamb, I would like to poison Niulang to death!"

这天，她狠一狠心，在白面饼里下了毒药，另外又烙了几张黑面饼，黑面饼里没下毒药，准备留给他们夫妻俩自己吃。嫂子老早在心中打好了如意算盘，这个傻牛郎别样事情都傻乎乎的，就是吃饭不傻，专拣好的吃，今天就让他去吃个够！

On that very day, she hardened her heart, and mixed some poison in the flour while she was making the pancakes. At the same time she made several poisonless ones especially for her husband and herself. "Though a fool in other things, Niulang isn't a fool in eating. Every time he just picks up the best. Today I'd like to have him have enough!" the sister-in-law calculated.

嫂子的心计哪能瞒得过老牛？这回，老牛又开口说话了："牛郎，今天你可要多留个心啦。晚点儿回去，到了家里可别吃白面饼，那里头有毒。你就专拣黑面饼吃吧。"

However, how could the sister-in-law's calculation conceal the ox? Now he was speaking to Niulang again, "Niulang, today you need to keep alert. Let's be home a little bit late. When you are back, remember not to eat the white pancakes. There is poison in it. You just pick up the black pancakes."

晌午时分，牛郎牵着牛回到家里，拿起一块黑面饼就吃。嫂子连忙过来，夺下他手里的黑面饼，顺手递过去一块白面饼："傻蛋，自家人还客气个啥，吃白的！"

At midday, Niulang came back home with the ox. When he arrived at home, he picked up the black pancake and began to eat. The sister-in-law came up hastily and seized the black pancake and gave him a white one instead, “You fool! We are but one family! Do not stand on ceremony. Eat the white pancake!”

“唉，白面的不多，嫂子您在家做饭也够辛苦的，你吃吧。”说着，牛郎又硬把白面饼往嫂子嘴里塞。

“There are not many white pancakes here. You have been busy cooking all day at home and very tired. You deserve the good cakes!” Niulang responded while pressing the white pancakes back to his sister-in-law.

他们两人正在那里推推让让，他哥哥正好从院子里进来，他不知底细，开口就说：“哈哈，今天太阳西边出啦，还从来没看见你们两人这么客气过呢。你们都不吃，我吃。”

Just when the two were trying hard to decline the offer, the elder brother passed by the courtyard. He was all blind to what was happening here. Then he said, “Hey! It seems that the sun rises from the west! I have never seen you two be so polite to each other. If no one eats it, I will!”

哥哥过来，夺过那白面饼就往自己的嘴里塞。嫂子一见，可急坏了，当着牛郎的面，又不能明说，只好把眼一瞪，蹿过去夺下那块饼，“啪”的一声就摔在了地上。说时迟那时快，蹲在屋里的那条小黄狗看见扔下来一块白面饼，顿时眉开眼笑，来得正好。“哈哈，今天主人开恩，给我改善伙食啦！”它连忙蹿过去，一口叼起白面饼，撒腿就往外跑，跑到院子里，一不小心又掉下来一小块。正好过来一只老母鸡，老实不客气，来个见者有份，也叼了去。

The elder brother came up, seized the white pancake and was about to put it into his mouth. Seeing this, the sister-in-law was very anxious. At the presence of Niulang, she could not reveal the truth. She glared at her husband, rushed and grabbed the pancake, and threw it to the ground with a poop. Just at this moment, a yellow dog that had been crouching in the house saw the pancake thrown at him, he was beamed with delight, “How lucky I am today! I will have a great meal!” He jumped up, held the pancake in his mouth and hurried to the courtyard. Unheedingly, a small piece was left over. At this moment an old hen passed by. She did not want to pretend to be polite, either. She hurriedly picked it up.

谁知道不一会儿工夫，那小黄狗和老母鸡就都把腿一伸，咽了气。

Guess what? After a while, both the little yellow dog and the old hen stretched their legs, dead.

这一下，可不得了！嫂子要害死牛郎的事情也就露了馅了。

哥哥的脸又往哪儿搁去？你这么大个事怎么也不跟我商量商量？往后教我怎么出去做人？哥哥越想越生气，越想越恼火，拽住媳妇就打。

The scheme that the sister-in-law wanted to poison Niulang to death was then exposed. The elder brother thought that his wife did really go too far. “Where may I hide my face? How may I explain to the villagers? Why don’t you talk it over with me at first?” The more the elder brother thought, the angrier he became. Then he pulled over his wife, and started to hit her.

牛郎看不过去了，走过去把哥嫂拉开，含着眼泪说：“哥嫂把我拉扯大，也不容易。咱们趁早分开过吧，省得我让嫂子给害了。”

Niulang could not pretend that he did not notice it. He came up and tried to pull them apart. With tears in his eyes, he said, “It is not easy for you to bring me up. Let’s divide the family as soon as possible. Otherwise, I will surely be poisoned to death.”

其实哥哥心里也老是想着要分家，就是说不出口，如今是牛郎先说的要分家，正好顺坡下驴。分家就分家，迟早是要分的，迟分不如早分。

The division of the family was exactly what the elder

brother had been longing for. But for the sake of the face, he did not put it forward first. Now that Niulang did this, he would not like to let this chance go. He agreed with Niulang by saying that division of the family was a matter of time. As it would come sooner or later, why not earlier?!

牛郎的舅舅听说了，过来一看，心里憋闷，这不是明摆着牛郎要吃亏了吗？牛郎傻乎乎的，连个老婆也还没有，光棍一个，让他往后怎么过日子？不过要让哥哥老是这么帮他，嫂子又不答应。俗话说，“家家有本难念的经”，这不是，摊上了，躲也躲不过去的。舅舅叹了口气，对牛郎说：“牛郎，你也别急，兄弟早晚要分家，这也是没办法的事。分就分吧，怎么着也是干活吃饭，你要是实在过不下去，就先到我家住一阵子吧。”说罢，抹一把眼泪，走啦。

When the uncle from their mother's side heard of this, he came over, too. He knew clearly in his mind that Niulang would suffer losses. Anyway, Niulang was a still bachelor without a wife. Who would take care of him? What's more, he was but a fool. How would he manage to live? But if the elder brother would go on helping him, the sister-in-law would never consent. There is an old saying, "Every family has its own thorny affairs". If it was true, then none could really escape. The uncle said to Niulang with a sigh, "Niulang, take it easy! Sooner or later the family should be divided. There is no other way. Whatsoever, it is just eating and working. If you'd think it is too harsh for you, you may move to our house to live together with us for some time." After he finished this, he wiped his tears and left.

到了外边，老牛又开口说话了："牛郎，你哥嫂要跟你分家，分就分。你别的东西全不要，就要上我和破车、疙瘩绳。"

While they had gone out of the house, the ox spoke again to Niulang, "Niulang, if your brother and sister-in-law ask you to divide the family, you may agree with them. Don't ask for anything but the broken ox cart, the knotty rope and me."

牛郎点点头说："行，我都听你的。"

"O.K. I will listen to you." Niulang said with a nod of his head.

到了分家这一天，舅舅来了。又是房子又是地的，一样一样都算计了一番，舅舅说："亲兄弟，明算账。二一添作五，就对半分吧。"

On that day when division had to be made, their uncle also came. Things to be divided included rooms, fields, and a lot of other properties. The uncle said, "Though you are brothers, it needs to be calculated clearly. Let's divide everything into halves."

他嫂子一听，当场就嚷了起来："不行不行，哪有这种分法的？你到村里去打听打听看，我们这个家，还不是全靠着我们夫妻两人一滴血一滴汗这么挣下来的。他一个傻蛋，啥也不会干，净让人家伺候他，到头来倒要来个对半分，有这种道理的吗？再说了，就是按人口分，也该是我们夫妻俩得二股，他才一股嘛，哪能分给他这么多？我不服，我就是不服！"

At this, the sister-in-law cried out, "How come! You may ask the villagers! This family was set up solely on our couple's perspirations and blood. He is but a fool. He does nothing but wait to be served. How can he ask for half of the property? Even it is divided by heads; we two should get two shares. He gets one! How can he receive so much? I don't agree! I don't agree at all!"

牛郎出来打圆场了："别吵别吵，一家人别伤了和气。我什么都不要，就要这头老黄牛、那辆破车，还有一根疙瘩绳。别的全归你们好了。"

Then Niulang stood out to make peace. He said, "Don't quarrel, please! We are still one family. Do not hurt each other. I don't want to have anything but the yellow ox, the broken ox cart and the lump rope. Everything else you may have them all."

说完，扭头就朝外走。

Then he turned around and left.

他嫂子不好意思了，连忙奔过来拉牛郎，假惺惺地说："咳，你也不拿上些粮食？"

A little bit embarrassed, the sister-in-law ran over and pretended, "Hey! Don't you want to have some grains?"

"不要不要。"

"No! No!"

"床上被褥总是要拿的吧。"

"Or bed things?"

"也不要。"

"No!"

说不要，就什么都不要。牛郎憋着一口气，拉起老牛，套上破车，喊一声"驾！"朝外就走。

He had said that he did not want anything else. So he really did not get anything else. Niulang breathed a deep breath, drew the old ox, put on the broken cart, cried a loud "Go!" and left for the outside.

舅舅过意不去了，谁见过有这么分家的？不行，不行，瞪了哥哥一眼，连忙追出门去：“牛郎，你给我回来，你又犯傻啦，快回来！”

The uncle felt very sorry, because he had never seen such a division like this before. “No, No!” he glared at the elder brother, and ran after Niulang, crying, “Niulang, come back! You fool, come back!”

牛郎头也不回，赶着牛就走：“你也不用管我，我走到哪算哪，天底下总有我牛郎立脚的地方。”

“Let me be! No matter where I go, I can make a living. I know there will surely be a place for me Niulang!” Niulang drove the ox forward without even looking back.

老黄牛跑得快，舅舅再也没追上。

The yellow ox ran so fast that the uncle could hardly catch up with them.

牛郎憋着一股劲赶牛车，到了三岔路口，就犯了傻，你说他该朝哪条路走呢?

The only thing that Niulang did was to drive the ox cart. But when he arrived at the crossroad, he was dumbfounded, “Which road shall I take?”

老黄牛当然明白牛郎的心思，就慢悠悠地对他说：“牛郎，你也不要着急，家都分好了，还怕啥？索性闭上眼睛先养养神再说吧。我会带你到一个好地方去的。”

It seemed that the yellow ox could read his mind. He said to Niulang slowly, “Niulang, don’t worry! Now that the family has been divided, what are you afraid of? Why don’t you close your eyes and repose for a while. I will take you to a beautiful place.”

牛郎早就把老黄牛当成是自己最亲最亲的亲人了，心一横，索性闭上眼睛，就让老黄牛给他带路。他们走啊走，走啊走，从早晨走到晌午，又从晌午走到太阳落山，眼看着天色一点点黑了下来，他们的牛车终于走进了一个山坳子里，那儿树木茂密，溪水潺潺，鸟语花香，很是幽静，就是前不着村，后不挨店的，看上去还有那么点儿荒凉。牛郎着急起来：“牛大伯，天都黑了，咱一天还没吃饭呢，怎么办？”

Niulang had already considered the old ox as his closest family member. So he made up his mind, closed his eyes, let the yellow ox lead him to wherever he wished. They walked and walked, from morning to midday, and from midday to dusk. When darkness fell, they discovered that they had arrived at a valley where the trees were flourishing; the streams were crystal clean; and the birds were singing and the flowers were fragrant. It was such a peaceful and quiet place! But Niulang started to become anxious since no villages and no people could be found around. He felt a sense of desolation indeed! So he said hurriedly to the ox, “Uncle Ox, it is dark now! We still have not eaten anything. What shall we do then?”

“不急不急，再拐个弯就到了，包你有吃有住，什么都不缺。”

“Don’t worry! After another turning, we will arrive at a place where you will never lack anything,” the ox replied.

果然，拐过一个弯，眼前就出现了一座大庭院。哈哈！好气派哇，青瓦白墙，高大门楼，还有一个好大好大的院子哩。老黄牛拉着车就闯进了门，对牛郎说：“到家了，还不快卸车。”

It was true that after another turning they arrived at a big courtyard. Alas! How fabulous! The green tile together with the white wall, the giant gate and building, and another gigantic courtyard, all made the building imposing! The yellow ox broke into the house with the cart, and said to Niulang, “It is home now. Hurry up! Unload!”

牛郎跳下车，先朝着屋里大声打了个招呼：“谁在家呀？”

Niulang jumped out of the cart, and greeted loudly to the house, “Anybody in?”

又喊了几声，静悄悄的就是没人答应，奇怪了，连忙问老黄牛：“怎么这家没有主人的？”

Nobody answered. It was all silent. Niulang felt [illegible] strange and he asked the yellow ox, “Why no host here?”

“嗨，这不就是你的家吗？”

“Why? Don’t you know that it is your home?!” the old ox said.

牛郎哈哈大笑起来，开什么玩笑？分家才分了一头牛、一辆破车，哪来这么好一幢房子？难道是天上掉下来的？不信，不信。

Niulang burst into great laughter at this. He said, “Are you kidding me? I got only an ox, a broken cart from the division of the family. Where can I get such a big house? Could it be possible that it is fallen from the Heaven? I don’t believe it. I don’t believe it at all.”

老黄牛却乐呵呵地对他说：“嗯，这个大庭院从今往后就归你了。这是老天爷给你的，别不好意思。你不是说饿了吗？快到厨房去看看吧，那儿什么好吃的都有。”

The yellow ox said to him merrily, “Yes, this big house belongs to you from now on. This is a gift from the Heaven. Don’t be shy. Just take it. Aren’t you hungry? Come to the kitchen to see if there is something to eat.”

牛郎不相信，进屋去转了一圈。哈哈，果然是吃的、住的、用的，样样都齐全了。牛郎做梦也没有想到过，还能有这么好一个新家。边上正好还有几亩荒地，就慢慢地开荒种地，过日子吧。

Niulang could not believe his eyes! He came into the house and was surprised to find that everything was there, things to eat, things to live with, and things to use! Everything! Niulang had never dreamed of having such a new and beautiful home. It was found later that there was a lot of land nearby waiting to be cultivated. Niulang could live on the land by planting.

从此以后，牛郎就在这个新家里住了下来。

Ever since, Niulang settled down at this new house.

二、池畔娶妻

2. Getting a Wife at the Pondside

牛郎有了新家，日子过得有滋有味的。过不了多久，他又跟老黄牛聊起天来：“牛大伯，你说这新家样样都好，可就是有些闷得慌，孤孤单单的，走进走出就我一个人，是不是？除了和你说说话，连个伴儿也没有。多寂寞！”

Having got a new house, Niulang was very happy. However, in a later chat with the yellow ox, he mentioned, “Uncle Ox, you know, everything is coming up at this home, but I feel a little bit bored and lonely. I am the only one person in and out of the house. I have got no one to talk to except you. How lonely I am!

老牛心里明白得很，乐呵呵地说：“你是想娶个媳妇了吧？嗯，年纪倒也是不小了，该成家了。”

The ox knew exactly what was in his heart. He said cheerfully, “Are you thinking of having a wife? Yes, maybe you are right. Since you are not young any more, you do need a family.”

牛郎低下头，不好意思地笑了起来。

Niulang lowered his head, smiled with embarrassment.

老牛从嘴里吐出一粒豆子，对牛郎说："把它种下去吧。"

Then the ox spit a seed out of his mouth, and said to Niulang, "Plant it in the field!"

牛郎把豆子种在大门口，浇上水。第二天，豆子芽苗就出了土；第三天，又爬起了藤。牛郎给豆子搭了个棚，没几天工夫，豆藤就把棚子全给爬满了，绿荫荫的好大一片。

Niulang planted the seed in front of his house, and watered it. The second day it shot up. The third day the rattan crawled up. Niulang built a canopy for it. Days later, the bean rattan covered the whole canopy, with a green shade under it.

老黄牛说："到了半夜三更，你就躲在豆棚底下看天上的仙女吧。天上的仙女可漂亮呢，这时候她们都能看得见你。谁要是连着偷看你七个夜晚，她就是想做你的媳妇了。到时候，我会帮你去娶她的。"

The yellow ox said to Niulang, "When midnight comes, hide yourself under the bean canopy to watch the fairies. The fairies in the Heaven are very beautiful. They can see you then. If there is somebody who watches you for seven nights on end, she will be your would-be wife. Then, I will marry you two."

夜深了，牛郎钻到豆棚底下，一眼不眨地朝天上望去。果然，他看见了七个仙女在天上的玉池边上游玩。这七个仙女，一个比一个长得漂亮。临走的时候，那个年纪最小的仙女偷偷转过身来向牛郎看了一眼，就又赶紧走了。

Late at night, Niulang entered into the canopy. He watched into the sky without even blinking his eyes. Eventually he saw seven fairies playing in the Jade Pond. All the seven fairies were breathtaking beauties. Before they left, the youngest turned around and looked at Niulang stealthily and left in a haste.

第二天夜里，牛郎还是钻到豆棚底下去看仙女，又看到了七个仙女在天上的玉池边上游玩。临走的时候，年纪最小的仙女又偷偷转过身来朝牛郎看了一眼，听到前面的仙女在喊她，只好慌慌张张地跟着走了。

The second night, Niulang got into the canopy again to watch the fairies. He again saw the fairies playing in the Jade Pond . Before they left, the youngest one turned around and looked at Niulang another time. Until she heard shouts from behind her, she had to leave in haste.

第三天，第四天，第五天，第六天，第七天，天天都是这样。天上那个仙女转身看牛郎的时间，一天要比一天长。看上去，她大概是看上牛郎啦。牛郎看那仙女，也一天比一天看得清楚，他的心里美滋滋的，老是在想，能娶上这么个漂亮的媳妇，该有多好！

For the next seven days it was all like this and the time the fairy spent on watching him was longer and longer day by day. It seemed that she had formed a liking for Niulang. Niulang also held similar feelings for her. He always thought how good it might be if he could marry such a beautiful fairy.

这天，老黄牛又开口了："牛郎，明天是七月七，南天门要开啦。南天门一开，天上那七个仙女就会下到我们这儿的河里来洗衣服。你知道她们是谁吗？她们全是王母娘娘的外孙女，长得可漂亮哩。年纪最小的那个仙女就叫织女，她不是已经看上你了吗？我来教你个好办法，你早早的就去躲在河边，趁她们不防备的时候，把织女晾着的衣服偷偷拿过来，千万不要还给她。这样一来，她就可以做你的媳妇啦。不过你千万要记住，将来她一定会向你讨衣服的。你还衣服的时候，一定要先叫三声'老牛'，等我来了，你再把衣服还给她。"

One day, the yellow ox started to speak to Niulang, "Niulang, tomorrow is July the seventh. The South Gate of the Heaven is going to be opened. The seven fairies will descend and come to the Pond to wash their robes. Do you know who they are? They are the granddaughters of Empress Wang in the Heaven. They are all very beautiful. Have you noticed that the youngest, who is a skilled seamstress, has a liking for you? I will tell you what to do then. Go out early in the morning and hide yourself behind the pondside, and then steal the robe of this maiden without being noticed by her. Remember: do not return the robe to her! Then she will become your bride. But you should keep in mind that she will surely ask you for the robe back. You should not return it to her until you call my name 'old ox' three times. Then I will come and it will be the time for you to return the robe to her."

牛郎一听，高兴极了。他一夜没睡着觉，睁大着眼睛就等南天门开。

At this, Niulang was extremely excited. He did not even dare to close his eyes for the whole night. He kept his eyes open waiting to watch the South Gate to be opened.

果然，到了半夜里，南天门"哗啦啦"一声响，开啦！黑咕隆咚的天空里顿时闪过一道亮光，从南天门飞出来七只鸽子，雪白雪白的，好看极啦，扑棱棱一阵响，鸽子全落在了离牛郎家不远的河边。一霎工夫，七只鸽子就变成了七个漂漂亮亮的大姑娘，有说有笑的，坐在河边的石头上洗起了衣服。洗好了衣服，晾在河边的石头上，又下河洗澡去了。

When midnight arrived, the South Gate was really opened with a crash-bang! A brilliant light suddenly shone onto the dark sky. Out of the South Gate swooped down seven doves, white and bright. They were so beautiful! The doves plopped down on the pond nearby the house of Niulang. Within the time of just a blink of eyes, the seven doves changed into seven beautiful girls. They sat alongside the Pond and started to wash their robes, singing and laughing at the same time. After that, they basked their robes on the stones beside the Pond, and jumped into the Pond to have a bath.

牛郎悄悄地过去，看准了她们中间年纪最小的那个姑娘，趁她一不留神，就偷偷地把她晾着的衣服给拿了过来。

Niulang went to the pondside on tiptoe. Making sure it was the robe of the youngest; he picked it up stealthily and hid it up.

这姑娘就是织女，其实她也早就看见牛郎了，不是说前些日子她已经偷偷地看牛郎，一连看了七夜吗？说起来，织女在天上，日子倒也是过得挺舒服的，谁不知道天上是神仙住的地方，不愁吃，不愁穿，山珍海味，绫罗绸缎，要啥有啥。不过话又说回来，那儿毕竟太寂寞了，哪有人间这么热闹！再说了，王母娘娘虽然很喜欢她的外孙女，却是样样事情都要自己来管的，从头管到脚，一点点芝麻绿豆的事情，她都得管，管得可严哩。外孙女的婚姻大事，更是全由她一人说了算，根本不管外孙女愿意不愿意。那个玉皇大帝，就更加别提了，整天板着个脸，从来没见他笑过，还动不动就发脾气，谁见了都怕。时间一长，外孙女一个个都觉得心里烦，都想着要下凡，要自己去寻找幸福，寻找快乐。所以她们到玉池游玩的时候，就总是忍不住要偷偷朝人间多看上几眼。是啊，虽然说人间也很清苦，哪有天上神仙逍遥？不过看起来他们却一个个活得都很开心，有的耕田种地，有的纺纱织布，有的上山砍柴，有的下河捕鱼，全靠自己一双手，劳动致富，这不是很好嘛。织女前些日子偷偷看牛郎，就是想找一个她看得上的小伙子。她觉得牛郎这个小伙子心地善良，又爱劳动，的确是个好人，就有心要下凡来帮他一把。如果两个人能够相亲相爱，生活在一起，那又有多好！现在她眼梢一带，早就看见牛郎偷走了她的衣服，顿时满脸通红，一颗心"怦怦怦"跳个不停，连忙大声喊叫起来："你还我的衣服，还我的衣服！我的衣服你怎么可以随便拿去呢？"

This girl was the Weaving Maiden, Zhinu. Actually she had paid attention to Niulang long before. Do you remember that it was she who had watched secretly at Niulang for seven days before? Actually Zhinu had had a very comfortable life in the Heaven. As legend goes, the Heaven was the place for the fairies to live. There was no need to worry about what to eat and what to wear there. The faires ate all the delicacies and wore the most beautiful clothes. They could have whatever they wanted. However, in the Heaven it was just too lonely a place for the fairy maidens. At least life there was not as lively as they believed it was on the Earth. Besides, though Empress Wang adored her granddaughters very much, she would like to make all the decisions for them, from the head to the toe, almost everything, no matter how trivial it might be. She was especially absolute when it came to their marriages, regardless of their own likes and dislikes. As to Jade Emperor , there was nothing better about him either, the granddaughters thought. He was such a tyrant that he always held a sullen face. No one had ever seen him smile before. He was easy to be irritated and quick-tempered. Everyone was afraid of him while they saw him. With the passage of time, the granddaughters were all thinking of leaving for the Earth and seeking their own happiness. When they came to the Jade Pond to play, they could not help glancing at the Earth stealthily for longer and longer moments. Yes, it was true that life on the Earth was much more bitter compared with that of the Heaven, but people there were much happier. Some were planting in the field while others were spinning and weaving; Some were chopping the wood while others were fishing by the riverside. They pursued their happy lives with all their own hands. That was exactly what the Heavenly fairies were dreaming of . The other day the Weaving Maiden, Zhinu, watched Niulang for quite a while because she really wanted to seek a man like him. She considered Niulang as kind-hearted and industrious. He was surely a man of her heart! So she decided to come down from the Heaven to help him. If they two could love each other, and live together, how beautiful life would be! Now she was looking out of the corners of her eyes and saw that Niulang had taken away her robe. Her face suddenly became blushed and her heart beat faster, then she cried out hurriedly, "Return my robe to me! Return it to me! How can you take away my robe!"

牛郎当然不会把衣服还给她的。老黄牛早就对他说过了，要娶织女做媳妇，你就不能还她衣服。牛郎打心底里喜欢上了织女，他一点儿也不傻，这可是个千载难逢的机会，怎么可以轻易放过了？所以他说什么也不会把衣服还给织女的。

Of course, Niulang would not return her robe to her. The yellow ox had told him in advance that if he wanted to marry the maiden, he should not return her robe to her. Niulang liked Zhinu from the bottom of his heart. At this moment he was not a fool at all! This opportunity was once in a blue moon. How could he let it go? So he determined not to return the robe to her.

织女也知道牛郎的心思，不过她喊还是要喊的。说起来，七姐妹一块儿出的南天门，怎么一个妹子不回去了？为啥不回去？这都得有个交代是不是？她这一喊，几个姐姐都听见了，她们回去不就可以交代了吗？

Zhinu also knew what Niulang was thinking about, but

she had to utter a crying. After all, when the seven sisters left the South Gate, they were all together. If she were not to go back, what would they have to report to the family? What would be the proper reason? It did need a sound excuse, yes? Once the sisters heard her crying, they might give an account for it.

果然，织女这一喊，六个姐姐全听见啦。正好，她们洗的衣服也都快要晾干了，赶紧一个个都穿上衣服，准备回天上去。她们一边穿衣服，一边回头催织女："织女，你怎么还不走？你到底还回不回去？"

Surely her crying had reached into the ears of her six sisters. It happened that all of their robes had been dried up. They hurriedly dressed themselves up and headed for the Heaven. While they were putting on their robes, they urged their sister, "Sis, speed up! Don't you want to come back?"

"织女，快回去吧，给外公外婆知道了可不得了！"

"Sis, hurry up! If our Granny knows this, we will surely die."

织女哭丧着脸说："我的衣服没有了，怎么回去呀？"

Zhinu cried, "Without the robe, how can I go back home?"

刹那间，六个姐姐都又变成了白鸽，“扑棱棱”飞走啦。快飞到南天门的时候，她们重新回转身来叫：“好妹妹，快回来吧。南天门要关啦，你快回来吧！”

All of a sudden, the six sisters changed back to be the doves and flopped their wings and flew away for the Heaven. When they were almost near the South Gate, they were still looking back and crying, “Dear sister, come back please! The South Gate will be shut soon. Do come back!”

从南天门里出来个红脸大汉，拉开嗓门吼着：“南天门要关啦，该回来的就快回来吧！”

From behind the South Gate, there came a giant guy with red face. He extended his voice and shouted loudly, “The door is closing now. He who wants to be back, be back!”

织女朝那边喊了一声：“我不回去了，你关吧。”

“I won’t be back. You shut the door.” Zhinu shouted back from the other end.

果然，只听得“轰隆隆”一阵响，南天门关上了。

The door of the South Gate indeed was snapped with a bang.

织女见南天门关了，六个姐姐也全飞走了，只剩下自己一个人，又没了衣服，只好躲在冰冷的河水里，好不狼狈！她忽然觉得心里有些空落落的，忍不住就淌下了眼泪。再一看，牛郎抱了她的衣服正要想跑，不觉心里一急，连忙喊了起来："回来！回来！你怎么抢了人家的衣服就跑？"

Seeing that the door of the South Gate was closed and all her six sisters had flown away, Zhinu suddenly felt a deep sense of loneliness and helter-skelter. Without her robe, she had to hide herself in the cold water. Suddenly she felt the emptiness in her heart and her tears started to stream down from her cheeks. At her second glance, she saw Niulang running away with her robe. In a hurry, she cried, "Come back! Come back! How can you run away with my robe?"

牛郎不好意思了，停住脚步，转过身来。织女正要想站起身去追他，一见牛郎在看她，吓得连忙又躲进水里去，只露出一个头，羞答答地说："大哥，快还我衣服！"

Niulang was embarrassed. He halted his steps and turned around. Zhinu wanted to chase after him, but sensing that Niulang was looking at her, she was embarrassed and had to hide herself under the water again with only her head exposed above the water. She said shyly, "Big brother, please give me back my robe!"

"给你衣服？这好办，你得先答应嫁给我。你愿意嫁给我，我才还给你衣服。”

“Give you back your robe? Good! But you must promise me that you will marry me at first. If you are willing to marry me, I will give it back to you,” Niulang said.

“大哥，求求你啦，你快还给我吧！水里好冷呀！”

“Please! Big brother. I beg you. Give it back to me! The water is chilly.” Zhinu begged.

牛郎把织女的衣服拿在手里晃了一晃：“是这件吗？”

Niulang waved Zhinu’s robe in his hands, and said, “Is it this one?”

“是的。”

“Yeah.” Zhinu responded.

织女往上一蹿，要去接衣服。牛郎不给她衣服，却高兴地说：“看见啦，看见啦！”

Zhinu attempted to jump out of water to catch the robe, but Niulang did not give it back to her. Instead, he said slyly, “I can see you now. I can see you now.”

吓得织女又连忙躲进了水里。

Zhinu was so scared that she had to hide under the water

again.

牛郎故意说:“啊！你不愿意嫁给我,那我可真的就要走啦。”

Niulang said with flirtation, “Ah? Don’t you want to marry me? Then I will have to go.”

织女满脸通红，只好羞答答地说：“好了好了，你这个人真坏！你就别闹了，把我的衣服还给我吧，让我穿上衣服，遮住身子，我一定到你家去，做你的媳妇，你说好不好？”

Already flushed in face, Zhinu said blashfully, “Well, you bad guy! Stop playing. Give me back my robe. Let me put it on and cover my body first. I will surely come to your house, and be your wife. Is that all right?”

好好好！牛郎见织女答应了，高兴得蹦了起来。不过他又想起了老牛叮嘱他的话，就多了个心眼，对织女说：“好妹子，你的衣服我会替你保管好的，你尽管放心。倒不如把我的衣服先脱下来给你穿，好吗？”

“That’s good!” Seeing that Zhinu had promised him, Niulang jumped out of joy. But when he recalled what the ox had told him before, he hurriedly added, “Dear sister, please don’t worry. I will take good care of your robe. I have an idea! I will take off mine, and you may have it on.”

织女红着脸，哪里肯答应，死活缠着牛郎，要讨还她自己那件衣服，后来看看牛郎一口咬定，就是不肯还，只好低着头说："那就听你的好了，快点把你的衣服给我。"

Red-faced still, Zhinu insisted that she do not accept his proposal. She wanted to have her own back. But when she realized that the chances of getting her own robe back were slim, and it seemed that Niulang was so determined that he would not give her robe back, she lowered her head and said, "Then I will listen to you. Give me yours quickly."

牛郎高兴极了，赶紧先把织女的衣服卷成一团，找了个十分隐蔽的地方藏了起来，然后脱下自己的衣服，扔了过去。

Extremely elated, Niulang rolled up Zhinu's robe quickly and hid it up in a secret and safe place. Then he took off his own robe and threw it to Zhinu.

织女穿上牛郎的衣服，磨磨蹭蹭上了岸，忸忸怩怩地说道："你这个人真是的。我都已经答应做你媳妇了，你还怕什么？快把我的衣服拿出来还给我，我一定会跟你走的。你看，南天门都关了，我还能上哪儿去？你要是还不放心，你只要拉着我的衣角不放，我就逃不掉了。"

With Niulang's robe, Zhinu dillydallied up to the bank. She said blushingly to Niulang, "What a person you are! I have promised you to be your wife. What are you still afraid

of ? Give me back my robe. I will surely follow you home. You see, the door of the South Gate has been shut. Where can I go now? If you still feel unsure of it, you may drag the corner of my robe. I've got nowhere to escape."

牛郎这时候可聪明了，他闷声不响，总是朝着织女笑，却就是不肯把她的衣服还给她，走过去一把拉住织女的手，就高高兴兴地回了家。

How clever Niulang had become this time! He did not speak much, but kept his smiling always! And he never returned her robe to her, either. He came up and took the hand of Zhinu, and went back home merrily.

老黄牛在一边看得清清楚楚，也称赞起牛郎来，好哇，牛郎这回可一点儿也不傻，你看，他不是把个漂漂亮亮的媳妇给领进门了吗?

Seeing crystal clear what was happening here, the ox praised Niulang, "Good Boy! You are not a fool at all! You see, now you are taking a beautiful wife home!"

抽个空挡，老牛又在牛郎的耳朵边上叮嘱起来："牛郎，可不能麻痹大意。你还得先找个地方把织女的衣服给藏好了，千万不能让她知道。你说是不是? 万一她要是知道了藏衣服的地方，说不定哪一天穿上衣服朝天上一飞，你这个媳妇不就没有啦。"

While Zhinu was absent, the yellow ox whispered to Niulang to warn him, "Niulang, keep your guard please! You need to find a place to hide her robe up. Do not let her know about it. Consider this: if she discovers the place where you hide the robe, she might put it on and fly back to the Heaven. Then you will have no wife."

牛郎走进走出，看了老半天，想来想去，总觉得家里这个庭院的里里外外，几乎没有一个地方是靠得住的。最后他终于想出来了一个办法，瞒着织女，就在自己的床脚底下挖了一个洞，再把织女的衣服包好，藏了进去。心想，我一年到头就睡在这件衣服的上头，还怕她会拿走吗？哈哈，这个办法太好了！织女她再聪明，也不会想到衣服就在她的床底下，是不是？

Strolling in the house back and forth, Niulang racked his brains to think out a place to hide the robe. After examining the courtyard inside and outside, he could not find a safe place. Later he worked out a way. Without the knowledge of Zhinu, he dug a hole under their bed, and rolled up her robe and then put it into the hole. He thought, "I will sleep in this bed year in and year out. Who may take it away? Great! It is a fantastic idea! Clever as Zhinu is, she will never get to know that her robe is just under her own bed!"

老黄牛点点头，又乐呵呵地对牛郎说："好哇！你把媳妇也领进门了，你也有房有地了，这个家没白分。明天你去把舅舅和哥哥嫂子他们都请来看看吧，再请上你的邻居们，让大家一起到这儿来聚聚，就赶紧把婚事给办了吧。”

The yellow ox nodded his head, and said to Niulang pleasingly, “Good! Now you have your own wife, your own land and your own house. You have not lost anything from the division of the family. Tomorrow you may invite your uncle, your brother and sister-in-law, and all your neighbors over, to have a good time and to finish the wedding ceremony.”

第二天，牛郎把舅舅、哥哥嫂子、街坊邻居全都给请来了。大家一看，嚯！这么漂亮的一个媳妇，还有这么气派的一个大庭院，牛郎真是交上好运啦！“六十年风水轮流转”，这话可一点也不假。嫂子一张脸涨得血红血红，在众人面前，她哪还敢说什么话？她实在是后悔死了。

The next day, Niulang did invite his uncle, his brother and sister-in-law and all his neighbors over. “Wow! Such a beautiful wife!” “Such a splendid courtyard!” “How fortunate Niulang is!” “What has Fate done to him?!” Those were the exclaimations. The face of his sister-in-law was reddened, too. In front of the crowd, she could say nothing but to feel shameful.

当着众人的面，牛郎和织女拜过天地，他们终于成了一家人啦。大伙儿在一起热热闹闹好几天。

At the presence of the audience, Niulang and Zhinu bowed before the Earth and Heaven as their witnesses of the marriage. Finally they became husband and wife. People gathered together and celebrated it for several days.

织女虽然是王母娘娘的外孙女，她却没有一点点架子，又勤劳，又温柔，真是百里挑一的好媳妇。她不但会养蚕，而且还会缫丝、纺纱、织绢，一有空闲，就上她的织机去织绢。织女织出来的绢可好哩，又细又软，又光又亮，那上面还有各种各样的花纹，比天上的彩云还要好看。附近的大嫂小妹知道了，大伙儿都赶过来向织女学织绢。

Being the granddaughter of Empress Wang in the Heaven, Zhinu, however, was not arrogant at all. On the contrary, she was industrious and gentle. She was one of the millions to be a good wife. She not only knew sericulture, but filature, spinning, weaving floret as well. As long as she had time, she would be seated in front of the loom to weave the floret. The floret that Zhinu wove was really very beautiful, soft and smooth, bright and brilliant, with various designs of flowers which were more beautiful than the colored clouds in the sky. The sisters and aunties in the neighborhood heard of this, and rushed to learn weaving floret from Zhinu.

从此以后，牛郎耕田，织女织布，他们相亲相爱，和和美美

的，小日子过得就比蜜糖都还要甜。后来，织女又生下了一男一女两个孩子，白白胖胖的，人见人爱，牛郎高兴得天天像过生日，张开嘴巴就想笑。

Ever since then, Niulang had been ploughing the field while Zhinu weaving the cloth. They loved each other, and lived a life which was much sweeter than the honey. Later, Zhinu gave birth to two babies, a boy and a girl, both lovely and lively. Niulang was extremely happy. For him, every day was like his birthday! Whenever he opened his mouth he could not contain his smiles.

大伙儿都非常羡慕牛郎，全都来向他打听，你这么好的一个媳妇，是从哪儿找来的？

People were all envious of Niulang and they came to pry on from where on earth he could get such a good wife.

牛郎指了指大门口的豆棚架，一五一十说出了这里边的根底。从此以后，豆子熟了的时候，姑娘们，小伙子们，大家争先恐后都会来这儿摘豆荚，拿回去种到他们自家的院子里。等到豆藤爬满架，他们就总是会拣个夜深人静的时候，一个个钻到豆棚底下去，向天上瞭望起来，人人都盼望着能够从这儿找到自己的幸福生活。

Niulang then pointed at the bean canopy in front of his house and revealed all his secrets. After listening to the story, boys and girls vied with each other to be the first one to come to Niulang's courtyard to pick up the beans and took them back home and planted them in their own yards. When the canopy was fully covered, they would like to choose a quiet night and entered into the canopy, looked up to the sky, hoping that someday they might also find their own happiness there.

三、织女思归

3. Nostalgia of Zhinu

一晃三年过去，两个孩子也会下地走路了。一家四口人的小日子过得甜甜蜜蜜的，人人都羡慕，可是他们却也有不称心的事。

Good times always fly! Three years passed quickly! The two kids of Niulang and Zhinu could walk on their own now. The family of four lived such a happy life that everybody admired it. However, they had their own worries and concerns sometimes.

什么事不称心？

What on earth made them worry?

织女不是从天上下来的吗？她想天上那个家了呀！

Do you remember that Zhinu was from the Heaven? She was missing her family in the Heaven now!

这天，织女涨红着脸对牛郎说："牛郎，你也知道，我的家在天上，我是从天上飞来的。那时候我还小，穿着外婆给我做的衣服，现在一晃三年过去了，不知道那件衣服还合不合身？你就拿出来再让我试一试嘛。咳，求求你啦，哪怕就是只让我看上那么一眼，我也甘心了。”

One day Zhinu said to Niulang with a reddened face, “My dear, you know, my home is in the Heaven. I am from the Heaven. When I left the Heaven, I was quite small then. I had the robe my grandmother made for me. Three years has passed, I wonder whether the robe still suits me. Will you please take it out and let me have a try. I beg you. Please! I will be very happy if you can even let me have a look at it.”

牛郎心里想，织女到了我家，一直待我这么好，恨不得把心都掏出来给我，如今她提出这么一点小小的要求，也不算太过分，我能忍心拒绝她吗？不过再一细想，这件事情可是非同小可的，老牛不是一再叮嘱过吗？别的事情样样都可以依她，就是这件衣服你千万不能给她。牛郎想到这里，真是一脸的尴尬，吞吞吐吐的，好说歹说，就是不肯把衣服拿出来。牛郎不肯把衣服拿出来，织女又有什么办法？她也不知道衣服藏在哪里，只好一个人躲在边上掉眼泪。

Niulang thought, “Ever since the day Zhinu arrived at my house, she has treated me quiet well. She loves me with all her heart. Now she is having such a minor request. It is not too much at all. How may I reject her? But how can I neglect the ox’ warning? I would like to give her anything but her robe!” He was in a great dilemma and he was totally blind as to what to do! He hesitated for a long while but he still insisted that he should not return the robe to Zhinu. While, for the maiden, she had no alternatives if Niulang did not give her back her robe. She would never know where the robe was hidden, so she sat alone in the corner, weeping.

唉！人要是一有了心病，那可是任什么药也没法治的。从此以后，织女就老是神思恍惚，闷闷不乐，干起活来丢三落四，就像掉了魂似的，饭也吃不香，觉也睡不好，愁眉苦脸，眼泪汪汪，一天到晚缠着牛郎，就是要想再看一看她自己的那件衣服。

Ouch! When a person suffers from the sickness of the heart, no medicine can cure it. Ever since then, Zhinu had been in a trance all the day along. She was so depressed and downcast as if she had gone out of her mind. She did not eat well. Nor did she sleep well. Every day she was weeping. From morning till night she was entangled with it and begged Niulang to give back her robe.

牛郎看着织女被这事折磨得面黄肌瘦，一副可怜巴巴的模样，他心里也是不好受哇。毕竟是相亲相爱的夫妻，哪能这么伤人家的心？到头来，牛郎的心也终于软了，叹一口气，对织女说："今天我就依你一回，不过你得先到门外去喂鸡，待一会儿，让我安排好了，会喊你进屋的。"

Niulang was also wrestling in his mind and felt greatly sympathetic for Zhinu especially when he saw Zhinu emaciated and pitiful. After all, they were an affectionate couple. Who would like to break the heart of his lover? At last, his heart was softened, and said to Zhinu with a sign, "Today I will fulfill your wish. But you must go out of the house to feed the chickens first. After a while, till I have arranged everything, I will call you in."

织女不知道他葫芦里卖的什么药，乖乖地去喂鸡了。牛郎见她已经走得老远，这才放了心，偷偷关上房门，搬开床铺，从床脚下的洞里取出那件藏了三年的衣服。一看，这衣服还是崭新的，一点儿也没损坏，这才重新搬回床铺，把一切都安排妥当了，喊织女进屋，又关上门，小心翼翼地把这件衣服拿出来给她看。

Zhinu could not figure out what he was trying to do. She had to obey his demands by going out to feed the chickens. Seeing to it that Zhinu had gone further away, Niulang was relieved. He quietly fastened the door and moved away the bed, from under which he took out the robe that had been hidden for three years. The robe was still brand new without any damage at all. He unfolded it on the bed. Making sure of all the arrangements, he called Zhinu back into the room, shut the door and cautiously he displayed her robe to her.

织女一见这件衣服，心情非常激动，眼泪忍不住就"簌簌"地流了下来。这件衣服是她从小穿着长大的，她怎么会不思念呢？她原想穿上衣服就立刻飞回天上去看望她的家人，不过一看四周的情形，房门关得紧紧的，又能从哪里飞出去呢？再说了，牛郎的一双眼睛这会儿正瞪得老大老大，一眨不眨地看着她，她也不忍心走哇。织女抖抖索索地穿上衣服，上看下看，前看后看，磨磨蹭蹭老半天，一张脸涨得血红血红，到头来终于不忍心走，又把衣服重新脱了下来，小心翼翼地还给牛郎，千叮万嘱，嘱咐他把衣服保管好。

The robe stirred up the excitement inside of Zhinu. Tears could not help streaming down from her cheeks. Ever since her childhood, the robe had been with her. How could she stop thinking of it? Now how much she wished that she would put on the robe and fly to the Heaven to meet with her family! But looking around, she found the doors were deadly fastened. Where could she fly to? In addition, the eyes of Niulang were broadly widened, without even a blink. How could she leave him? Zhinu then put on the robe with a tremble, and then examined it from the back to the front, from the top to the foot, for about half a day with a reddened face. Eventually, she decided to take off the robe and with great cautions she returned it to Niulang, telling him again and again that he should take good care of it.

又过了十多天，织女心里头那个想家的疙瘩还是解不开，实在没办法，只好又缠着牛郎，要看看那件衣服。

About ten days later, the robe was still in Zhinu's heart and she dwelt on it almost every day. She had no other way but to pledge Niulang to let her have another look at the robe.

牛郎的心里也不好受哇，他不会兜圈子，就直统统地把底牌摊了出来："咳，万一你穿上衣服，扑棱棱飞回天上去了，撇下我和两个孩子，可怎么过日子呀？"

Niulang felt upset too. He did not know how to go around the topic. Instead, he laid cards in the table and said, "Dear, if you put on the robe and with a flap you fly to the Heaven, leaving me and the two kids alone, how can we live without you?"

话都说到这个份上了，织女一咬牙，也说出了心里话："牛郎，你待我这么好，我怎么会不知情呢？不过你看人家，哪家媳妇不回娘家去看看的？爹妈从小把我拉扯大，我如今回去看看他们，这也是应该的嘛。你说是不是？如今倒好，自从那回出了南天门，我离开爹妈都三年多了，居然还没有回去过一趟，也不知道他们有多想我呢？还有外公、外婆，还有我的六个姐姐，他们可都是我的亲骨肉哪！三年来，我哪天不在梦里想着他们？梦醒了，就又什么也没有了。你说我心里苦不苦？让我上天去看看他们，这可是一点儿也不过分的吧？"说到这里，织女忍不住又簌簌地流下了眼泪。

Zhinu clenched her teeth and determined to speak out

her mind too, "Niulang, I do know that you are good to me. But if you look at the daughters-in-law in other families, you may see that there is no one who doesn't return to their own family to visit their parents. My mother and father brought me up ever since I was born. Now I would like to go to visit them. It's quite normal, isn't it? But now you see, ever since I left the South Gate, I've never been home again. It has been three years! Do you know how much they may miss me? I have also my grandparents and other six sisters. All of them are my own flesh and blood! It has been three years! How can I stop thinking of them in my dreams? Every time when I woke up, everything disappeared. Can you understand how bitter it is? Let me be back to the Heaven to have just a look. Do you think it is too much for me?" She wept intensively while she was speaking.

牛郎说："哪家媳妇不回娘家？不过你要是走了不回来，两个孩子都还这么小，教我一个人可怎么把他们带大呀？"

Niulang said, "No daughter doesn't visit her family. But I wonder if you leave us, will you return? We have two small kids. How may I raise them single-handedly?"

"不会的，不会的。虽说我是天女，不过既然已经跟你结成夫妻，我们是一定要白头到老，永不分离的。如今又生下这么好的一对儿女，我这个做娘的怎么会忍心撇下他们不管呢？你尽管放心好了，我一定会回来的。”

“No, no! Though I am a girl from the Heaven, I will not abandon you because we have been husband and wife. We will always live together and nothing can separate us. Not to mention that we have such a lovely pair of kids. As a mother, how can I bear to abandon them? Please take it easy, I will surely come back to be with you.” Zhinu assured him.

看着织女情真意切的神态，牛郎终于动了心，他一时糊涂，忘记了当年老牛的嘱咐，竟没有再去招呼老牛，就自作主张把衣服拿出来交给了织女。不过他毕竟还是有些担心，就站在房门口，牢牢守住房门。

Niulang was deeply moved by Zhinu’s sincerity. He fell into such a confused situation that he ignored all that the ox had told him before. Without getting any permission from the ox, he made up his own mind to return the robe to Zhinu. However, his heart was still unsettled. He stood at the door of the room trying to guard her from flying away.

织女一穿上这件衣服，小时候在天宫里的情景又一幕幕出现在她的眼前。她仿佛听见了亲人们在呼唤她的声音，她该怎么办呢？这时候，织女心乱如麻，泪下如雨，忍不住一阵心酸，走过去抱起自己的两个儿女亲了又亲。说起来，她也实在是舍不得孩子，舍不得牛郎，可是她又多么想马上就回天宫去看看，去看看她娘家的亲人。织女一边流泪，一边抱着孩子，在屋子里兜圈子。到后来，她终于横下一条心，咬一咬牙，把孩子朝床上一放，"嗖"的一声，就从窗口飞了出去，腾云驾雾，直奔南天门去了。

As soon as Zhinu put on her robe, all of the happy moments of her childhood in the Heaven were returned to her mind. It seemed as if she could hear her relatives calling her name from above the Heaven. What could she do now? She had mixed feelings, and her tears started to shed down from her cheeks. She walked over to kiss the two kids again and again. It was true that she did not want to leave them. She did not want to leave Niulang, either. But she did miss her family and did want to go back to just have a look. Zhinu circled around the courtyard unceasingly, with tears remaining in her face and the children held in her brace. Later, she clenched her teeth to make up her mind and put the pair of kids onto the bed, and with a whiz she flew away from the window, over the clouds and mists, for the South Gate of the Heaven.

牛郎哪里想到她还会有这一招？等到他清醒过来，要想扑过去拉住她的时候，早已经来不及了。他连忙转身出大门去看，这时候织女已经飞上了天空，只见她越飞越高，越飞越远，不一会儿工夫就无影无踪啦。

Niulang had never expected that she would do this. When

he came to, and attempted to drag her back, she had vanished into the distance. Hurriedly he came out to the house gate but only to see that Zhinu had left the Earth and flown for the sky. She flew higher and higher, farther and farther away, and soon was lost out of the sight of Niulang.

听得一对儿女在撕心裂肺地哭着喊娘，牛郎也忍不住掉下了眼泪，只好心急慌忙地去找老黄牛商量：“牛大伯，织女走啦。”

Hearing his children crying harshly searching for their mother, Niulang could not help crying, too. He hurried to the ox for an idea, “Uncle ox, Zhinu has left.”

老牛早就料到了这一步，倒也不着急：“你看你看，我早就提醒过你了不是，你为啥不先叫三声‘老牛’，等我来了，你再把衣服还给她呢？”

It seemed that it was all within the prophecy of the ox. He was as cool as a cucumber, and said unhurriedly, “You see, you see. Have I warned you before that if you want to give her the robe you should call ‘old ox’ three times?”

“是啊，是我一时莽撞，把你嘱咐的话给忘了。不过她临走时说过，她一定会回来的。”

“Yes. It’s my fault.” Niulang admitted, “I have forgotten what you have told me. But before she leaves, she has promised me that she will be back."

"你看你看，你又犯傻了不是？俗话说，天上一时辰，世间好几年。她在天上跟她家里人说几句话的工夫，也就够你等好几年啦，你一个人带着两个孩子，能挺得过来？再说了，她倒是想回来，她外公外婆还会放她回来吗？她外公是玉皇大帝，脾气可暴躁啦，谁斗得过他？"

"You see. You see. You are a fool again!" the ox said, "There's an old saying: 'A day in the Heaven, years on the Earth'. The time when she says a few words with her family, you need to wait on the Earth for several years! You are alone with the kids, how can you suppose to pull through? Again, even though she would like to come, will her grandparents allow her? Her grandfather is Jade Emperor. He is notorious for his bad temper. Who can fight against him?"

这一说，牛郎急得直跺脚。

At these words, Niulang jumped up with anxiety.

老牛却还是不着急，依旧慢悠悠地说："也没啥了不起的，你赶紧去追她吧。"

However, the ox wasn't in a hurry at all. He kept his even voice and said, "Nothing is serious. Why don't hurry up and chase after her?"

“啥？我去追？她是腾云驾雾上的天，我一个凡人怎么追？”

“What? Chase after her? She leaves with the clouds and mists. How can I, an earthly man, chase after her?” Niulang said.

“你把我杀了，披上我这张皮，就能上天了。”

“Kill me. Put on my hide, then you can fly to the Heaven.”

牛郎一听，吓得变了脸色，连忙双手乱摇：“不行不行，你是我的恩人，我怎么舍得杀你？我宁可自己吃苦受累，一个人把一双儿女拉扯大，也不能剥了你的皮去追她呀！”

When Niulang heard of this, he was so horrified that his face was transfigured. He waved his hands and said, “No, no! You are my savior. How can I kill you? I would rather suffer and toil and raise the two kids on my own than to kill you to chase after her!”

牛郎说的可全是实话。老牛待牛郎多好，这是牛郎一辈子也不会忘记的。要不是老牛，牛郎能过上这么好的日子吗？牛郎能娶上这么好的媳妇吗？牛郎能有这么好的一对儿女吗？牛郎今天过的日子，里里外外，上上下下，哪一件不全靠了老牛？牛郎报恩都还来不及呢，他能把恩人给杀了吗？不行不行，牛郎思来想去，别的事都可以做，就是这件事是万万做不得的。

These words were truly from Niulang’s heart. The ox had

been so dear to him. Niulang would never forget his kindness. "If it were not the ox, how could I Niulang live such a happy life? How could I Niulang marry such a nice wife? How could I Niulang have such a pair of cute kids? Is there anything that I Niulang have today, from inside the house to outside, from the top to the bottom, that is not from the ox? I am so grateful to him. How could I kill my benefactor? No, absolutely no!" He would like to do anything else but to kill the ox with his own hands.

老牛却不这么想。说起来，他的年纪也够大的了，总有一天是要死的。要是自己死了还能帮牛郎办成一件大事，那么他也就觉得值了，死也瞑目了。再说，牛郎可是他的恩人哪。想当年他老牛孤苦伶仃地躺在大山里，没有一个人来照料他，那个日子多难熬！后来幸亏来了个好心的牛郎，帮他治好了伤。从此以后他们就相依为命，相互照顾，这样一份情谊当然是永世难忘的。俗话说，"滴水之恩，涌泉相报"。如今他老了，要死了。这时候牛郎却偏偏遇上了难事，他要上天去找他的媳妇，他一个凡人，哪能上天？如果牛郎能披上他老牛的皮，就可以腾云驾雾上天了。在这个关口上，他老牛能不管吗？当然是要管的。老牛把自己的皮送给牛郎，这也就成了一件理所当然的事情啦。

However, the ox was not with him in this matter. He thought he was old enough. Sooner or later he should die. If he could help Niulang accomplish a great deed before his death, he would be very happy. It was worth the while. Furthermore, Niulang was his benefactor, too. He remembered the miserable days when he was lying in the lonely valley. No one came to visit him. It was this kind-hearted Niulang who cured him of his wounds. Ever since then they depended on each other, took care of each other. He would never forget this precious memory forever! There's a saying, "Graciousness of the water drop, the bubbling spring returns." Now that he was advanced in age, and his time on the Earth was not much. It happened that his host was facing such an emergent matter since he had to go to the Heaven to chase his wife back. How could an earthly man like him go to the Heaven? If Niulang could put on his hide, he would speed across the sky. At this critical moment, how could I, the ox, sit on? Of course, I should stand up and help him. The ox took it for granted that he should offer his hide to Niulang.

老牛左劝右劝，牛郎却死活不肯答应。到头来，老牛也发火了，一赌气，朝墙上猛一撞，"咕咚"一声，躺在地上，顿时就断了气，看你剥不剥皮？

No matter how hard the ox attempted to persuade Niulang, the latter did not let him do it. Finally, the ox was irritated. Rashly he hit himself onto the wall with a thump, then he lay down to the ground, dead. Niulang had no way but to peel off the hide.

牛郎号啕大哭，再也救不活老牛啦，怎么办？静下心来一想，事到如今，只好听老牛的话，剥下它的皮来救急了。他又去编了两个箩筐，再去找来一根黄杨木扁担，正好做成一副担子，一头担着儿子，一头担着女儿，再披上牛皮，一蹬腿，嘿！果然腾云驾雾的，飞了起来。

Niulang cried loudly. What could he do to save the ox? No way! He quietened his heart and thought that up to now he had to obey the ox – to peel off his hide and to use it in the emergency. He then came to plait two baskets, made a shoulder pole with the boxwood. Everything ready, with his son in one basket and his daughter in another, he then put on the hide of the ox. With just a stretch of his legs, he found himself really flying over the clouds and mists!

好了，牛郎又有办法了。于是他就挑着这副担子直奔南天门，要去追赶织女。

Thank goodness! Niulang finally found the way. Now with the burden he was heading directly for the South Gate to chase after Zhinu.

到了南天门一看，那里果然气势雄伟，光是那汉白玉的门柱子，就前后竖了三道，一道比一道高大，一道比一道把得严实，凡人哪里能进得去？到了头门，只见有一头金狮正蹲在那里把门，那金狮全身放着耀眼的金光，让人都睁不开眼睛。牛郎记住了老牛临死前嘱咐过他的那番话，不管三七二十一，挑着担子就往里闯。

When he arrived at the South Gate, he found that it was really splendid! Just look at the three gate pillars with white marble! One was taller and stronger than another. How could an earthly man like him enter it? A gold lion was crouching in front of the gate as the guard. With the dazzling golden light from all over its body, people could hardly open their eyes before him. Niulang recalled what the ox had told him before his death that no matter what would happen, he should break in boldly.

金狮看见牛郎要闯进来，当然不会答应，当即一声吼，龇牙咧嘴扑了过去。

Noticing Niulang's attempts to break in, of course the gold lion would not permit. With a loud roar, he pounced onto Niulang with the crunching teeth.

牛郎停住脚步，大声呵斥起来："嘿！谅你也不敢，你知道我是谁？我是你的七姑爷。你睁大眼睛仔细看，这不是两个穿红兜兜的娃娃？"

Niulang paused and berated him in a loud voice, "Damn

it! I bet you don't dare! Do you know who I am? I am the seventh brother-in-law. Open your eyes and have a look carefully. Aren't they the two babies with the red bellyband?"

金狮过来，看了又看，嗅了又嗅，喔，一点儿不错，这是织女的两个孩子，踫不得的，只好乖乖地躺下了。

The gold lion came up and looked and smelled up and down again and again and discovered that they were exactly the kids of Zhinu. He did not dare even to touch them and had to let them enter without much interference.

说着就到了二门，那里守着头银狮，银光闪闪，愈发觉得有些冷。这会儿，它正恶狠狠地瞪着大眼呢。

As they arrived at the Second Gate, a silver lion was guarding, with the shiny and chilly light of silver. At this moment, the silver lion was staring at them brutally with the sharp eyes.

牛郎当然不怕它，当门一站，又大声呵斥起来："嘿！谅你也不敢，你知道我是谁？我是你的七姑爷。你睁大眼睛仔细看，这不是两个穿红兜兜的娃娃？"

However, Niulang was not fearful at all. He stood there and abused him loudly, "Damn it! I bet you don't dare! Do you know who I am? I am your seventh brother-in-law. Open your eyes and have a look carefully. Aren't they the babies with the red bellyband?"

银狮过来，摇头晃脑地，看了又看，嗅了又嗅，嗯，一点儿不错，这是织女的两个孩子，得罪不起，只好又放他们过去了。

The silver lion came up and examined them thoroughly and smelt them from the back to the front. Finally he had to admit that they were the two kids of Zhinu. He did not dare to offend them, and had to let them go in.

到了三门，出来两个小鬼，面目狰狞，煞是可怕，闷声不响，举起手里的狼牙锤就朝牛郎劈了过来。

As they arrived at the Third Gate, two little ghosts jumped out abruptly. They were ugly and angry. Without being noticed they raised their wolf-teeth hammer and attacked Niulang.

牛郎停住脚步，瞪大眼睛喊了起来："哪来的野鬼，毫无一点规矩，敢来拦你七姑爷，你们睁大眼睛好好给我瞧瞧，这不是两个穿红兜兜的娃娃？"

Niulang halted his steps and yelled with his broad eyes, "You wild ghosts! Behave yourselves! Who dares to stop the seventh brother-in-law? Open your eyes and look at the two kids with the red bellyband?"

嚯，好大的口气！这人怎么没见过？那两个小鬼傻了眼，再走过来朝那担子里一瞅，果然是一男一女两个小娃娃，穿着一色的红兜兜，那两张小脸，活灵活现就像是王母娘娘。哎哟哟，大水冲了龙王庙，一家人不认得一家人啦！这不是织女的两个小孩儿吗？自家人，自家人，可不敢得罪了。

“Wow! What a tone! But we have never seen you before?” The two ghosts then came up and looked at the baskets and they indeed saw two babies, a boy and a girl with the red bellyband. Their little faces took after that of Empress Wang so much! “Ouch! It was a pity that we nearly missed identifying our family members! How could it be! Aren’t they the two kids of Zhinu? We belong to the same family! I do not dare to offend them.”

怎么办？两个小鬼一商量，赶紧先派一个进去报信，一个就拦在门口，点头哈腰地跟牛郎敷衍着，也不说让进，也不说不让进。

What to do then? After careful considerations, the two decided to have one go into the Heaven to send the message while the other held Niulang at the gate, perfunctorily talking with Niulang without giving him permission to enter.

不一会儿工夫，王母娘娘颤颤巍巍迎了出来。她心里头一百个不舒服，可是脸上却总还得装出笑脸来不是？

After a brief moment, Empress Wang came out quiveringly and loftily. She was very upset in her heart, but in her face she had to pretend a smile.

说起来，织女私自下凡，嫁给了牛郎，这件事她王母娘娘是坚决不答应的。非但王母娘娘不答应，玉皇大帝的火气就更大了。不过毕竟生米已经煮成熟饭，你们老俩口生气有啥用？你看，这不是，外孙女婿挑了一副担寻上门来，把两个小娃娃也给带来了，能不认吗？

The fact that Zhinu descended down to the Earth without their permission and the decision of marrying Niulang had annoyed Empress Wang very much. Not only was the Empress upset with it, Jade Emperor was even furious about it. Now that it had become the fact, what could they do to change it? You see, when the grandson-in-law came with the kids, they had no other way but to receive them.

不过，王母娘娘的鬼点子毕竟还是蛮多的，外孙女婿头一次上门，她就先要给他个下马威，只见她一边满脸堆笑，一边就把牛郎领进了一间屋子。

But to demonstrate her authority, Empress Wang decided to play a trick on Niulang first. After all, this was the first time for them to meet. She led Niulang into the room with smiles.

牛郎进屋一看，怎么在炕上坐着七个姑娘？原来这是织女和她的六个姐姐，只见她们全都长得一模一样，又穿着一色的衣服，正在那里低着头纳鞋底呢。

When Niulang entered the room, he was dumbfounded to find that there sat seven girls on the *kang*. Zhinu, along with the other six sisters, all of whom not only resembled in appearance, but wore the same colored robes, was working on the soles of the shoes.

王母娘娘朝炕上一指，不冷不热甩过来一句话："哪个是你媳妇？你自己认去吧。认准了你带走；认错了可别怪我。"

Pointing at the *kang*, Empress Wang said to Niulang in a lukewarm voice, "Who is your wife? You identify by yourself. If you can get it right, you may take her home; if not, please don't blame me, I will not let her go."

牛郎一个咯噔，想起老牛临死前的交代，连忙放下担子，让两个孩子上前去认娘。

Seconds later, he was reminded of words that the ox had told him before his death. He hurriedly put down his burden on the ground and asked the two kids to identify their mother.

哈哈，这办法可真灵。两个孩子还会不认得自己亲生娘的

吗？他们的脚一落地，就哭着直奔过去，扑进了织女的怀里。

And this worked! The kids knew their mother so well that when they were put onto the ground, they rushed to their mother with cries.

织女连忙伸出双手，抱住自己的亲骨肉，泪流满面，亲了又亲，害得边上的六个姐姐也都忍不住哭了起来。

Zhinu also stretched her hands to embrace her dear babies, crying with tears. She kissed them again and again. Her affection greatly touched the hearts of the other six sisters. They could not help crying with them altogether.

事到如今，王母娘娘还有什么办法？当着这么多外孙女的面，当着牛郎织女一家四口的面，她能说什么？只好叹一口气，扔下一句话来："手心手背都是肉。织女是我的外孙女，总不能亏待了她。既然都来了，就先住下再说吧。"

Up to now, what should Empress Wang do? At the presence of her granddaughters and the family of Niulang, what should she say? She said with a sigh, "You are all my flesh and blood! Zhinu is my granddaughter. I won't mistreat her. Now that you are here, settle down first."

王母娘娘吩咐下去，让底下的人给安排一间屋子，就让牛郎他们一家人先在天宫里住了下来。

Empress Wang ordered her retinues to arrange a place for the family of Niulang, and then they settled down in the Palace of the Heaven.

四、天宫斗法

4. Fighting in the Palace of Heaven

牛郎到了天上，见着什么都觉得新鲜，这里看看，那里看看，东转西转，整天咧开了嘴巴笑个不停。不过几天下来，他却又开始觉得浑身不自在起来了，为啥？原来他终于发现，这里的人原来都是不干活的，整天吃了玩，玩了吃，时间一长，这还有什么意思呢？所以一到晚上，他就在织女的耳朵边上唠叨起来："织女，这里可不是咱们两人呆的地方，咱们还是回老家去吧。到了老家，我耕田，你织绢，每天都有做不完的事，自己动手，丰衣足食，心里多踏实！天宫里的这种生活，我可过不惯。"

The first days when Niulang arrived at the Heaven, he found freshness in everything. He looked here and there, smiling every day. But soon he was tired of it. Why? Because he discovered that people here did not work at all. They ate and played and ate again. After some time, he thought there was no meaning in it. When evening came, he talked incessantly before Zhinu, "Zhinu, this is not the place for us to live. Let's go back to our home where I plough and you weave. We have a lot of things to do with our own hands. We will not lack anything! I am not used to the life here in the Heaven."

说起来，牛郎的这种想法，织女倒是完全可以理解的。想当初，她能够下决心去到人间，和牛郎结为夫妻，其实她也是这么想的。她总觉得天宫里的生活虽然舒服，却一点儿也不自由，也毕竟太寂寞了，哪有人间好？所以她宁可自己多吃点苦，也要和牛郎在一起，过一种自由自在、开开心心的生活。再说了，她和牛郎相亲相爱，如今又有了一对活泼可爱的孩儿，还有什么不满足的地方？她这次回到天上，是来看看爹妈，看看外公外婆和六个姐姐的，现在和他们都见过面了，说过话了，是也该跟牛郎一起回家去了。

Zhinu could fully understand the feelings of Niulang. Actually this was the very reason why she decided to come down to the Earth and marry Niulang. She thought that although life in the Heaven was much comfortable and easy yet it was restricted and lonely. It was not at all better than that of the Earth. So she would rather toil more to work together with Niulang, living a free and happy life. What's more, they loved each other, and they had a couple of kids. They were supposed to be contented. This time she intended just to pay a brief visit to her parents and grandparents and her six sisters. Now she had finished meeting with them, it was the right time for her to go back home with Niulang.

织女把这层意思跟爹妈说了，爹妈心疼自己的小女儿，从小一直都是对她百依百顺的，他们虽然有些舍不得织女走，最后倒也还是想得开的，说是既然你认准了要回人间，那就回吧，我们也不拦你。不过你还是先去跟外婆说一声的好，听听她的意思。说起来外婆也是最疼你的，是不是？

Zhinu explained what she thought to her parents. Though her parents adored their daughter very much ever since her childhood and did not want to let her go, finally they approved of her request by saying, "If you really like the life on the Earth, you may go back. We won't stop you. But before you go, you'd better ask for your grandma's permission first. After all, your grandma loves you most, don't you think so?"

于是，织女又去找她的外婆王母娘娘。王母娘娘一听织女说要回人间，连忙双手乱摇，颤颤巍巍地开了口："心肝宝贝，你可别来添乱。昨天你外公还跟我吵了一架呢。你外公这几天的脾气一直不顺，为啥？为来为去就为的是牛郎。不知道为啥？他总是对牛郎看不顺眼。我几次劝他，说牛郎有啥不好？他长得英俊，手脚又勤快，又知道疼咱们的织女，这样的外孙女婿，到哪里找去？岂不是要比天宫里的那些个男孩子强多了？可是你外公却不这么想，他指着我的鼻子就破口大骂，说我是头发长，见识短，说我婆婆妈妈，优柔寡断，哪像个王母娘娘的样子？照你外公的说法，这门亲事是门不当，户不对，玉皇大帝的外孙女怎么可以嫁给凡间一个放牛的穷人家孩子呢？这件事要是传出去，教他的老脸往哪儿搁？你说，在这个节骨眼儿上，你们说要回去，他能同意吗？他一发火，事情更加难办了。我劝你们还是先等几天吧。

你外公的为人，你也是知道的，看起来他正在想办法要害牛郎呢。这几天里，你要多长几个心眼，多提防着点，先帮助牛郎躲过眼前的难关，然后我们再慢慢想办法，好吗？”

As soon as Empress Wang heard that Zhinu wanted to go back to the Earth, she waved her hands unceasingly and said with a tremble, “My dear, stop making troubles! Yesterday I quarreled harshly with your grandpa. His temper has been quite hot these days. Why? It is because of Niulang. Reason? He did not like him. I tried to persuade him many times, saying Niulang is a good person, since he is handsome and hardworking and he loves you so much. Nowhere can we find such a nice grandson-in-law. And he is better than any other boy in the Heaven. But your grandpa doesn’t think so. He shouted abuses at me, saying I am short-sighted and hesitant and not empresslike at all. According to your Grandpa, this marriage was not at all a good match! How could the granddaughter of Emperor marry a poor earthly Niulang? If this were to spread out, where could he conceal his face? At this critical moment, if you say you would like to go back to the Earth, will he agree with you? If he becomes angry, it will be even worse. I admonish you that you wait a few more days. You know your Grandpa more than anyone else. It seems that he is going to do something to prosecute Niulang. For the following days, you should keep an eye on helping Niulang pull through the trouble. Then we will find a way out later, ok?"

织女听完外婆这番话，不觉心头一紧，就不再提回人间的事，先忙着回去和牛郎商量起对付外公的事情来。

At this, Zhinu felt greatly uneasy and she did not dare to mention any more that they would like to go back to the Earth. She hurried home and talked it over with Niulang as to how to deal with her grandpa.

这天，织女把房门一关，就小心翼翼地对牛郎说："牛郎呀，刚才听我大姐说，外公明天要和你赌输赢呢，这事儿可不好办，你得当心哪。他把自己藏了起来，再叫你去寻。你就慢慢地寻去吧，寻了屋里寻屋外，寻了东院寻西院，你把天宫寻个遍，到头来你寻到南墙根底下，那里正趴着一只大臭虫，那就是你外公变的。记住了吗？"

That day, Zhinu shut the door tightly and said to Niulang cautiously, "Niulang, just now I was told by my eldest sister that tomorrow my Grandpa will have a bet with you. This is really thorny. Keep your guard! He will hide himself up and ask you to seek him. You will seek him inside the house and outside the house, from the east to the west. After you have searched thoroughly in the Heaven, you will find a bedbug at the foot of the South Wall. This is the avatar of my Grandpa.

Clear?”

“记住了，记住了。”牛郎心里有数，外公要害自己，这事可不能麻痹大意。

“Yes, I do.” Niulang replied. He knew clearly that if the grandpa wanted to do harm to him, he should not lower his guard.

果然，到了第二天一清早，外公就找上门来了：“外孙女婿，今天我没事，咱俩做个游戏吧。”

The next day the grandpa really came to their house, and said to Niulang, “Grandson-in-law, today I have nothing to do. Let’s play a game.”

牛郎憨笑着说：“外公外公，你都胡子一大把了，还做游戏。说起来，你年纪大，我年纪轻，别人看见了都会说是我欺侮你，这事儿我可不能干。”

Niulang laughed naively, “Grandpa, Grandpa. You are old with the beard. Do you still like playing games? And you are old and I am young. People will say that I play tricks on you. I would rather not play.”

外公见他不敢玩，愈发放了心，连忙说：“不怕不怕，是我要跟你玩游戏的，谁敢说你？咱们玩捉迷藏吧，我藏起来，让你来寻。寻见了，我免你无罪；寻不见，哈哈，那就老实不客气，我就要吃了你。你敢不敢玩？”

The grandpa saw that Niulang didn't dare to play the game, his heart was settled and he said hurriedly, "Don't be afraid! It is me who wants to play games with you. Who dares to blame you? Let's play hide-and-seek. I hide. You seek. If you can seek me, I will pardon you; if you can't seek me, then I will not be polite. I will eat you up. Do you dare to play?"

“敢，有啥不敢？”

"I dare. Why not?" Niulang said.

“好，那你先把眼睛闭上，我藏好了就喊你。”

"All right. Close your eyes. Wait until I hide myself. I will call you later." The grandpa ordered.

牛郎刚刚把眼睛闭上，外公“嗖”的一下，变成了一只臭虫，悄悄地趴在了南墙根底下。

As soon as Niulang closed his eyes, the grandpa changed into a bedbug and hid himself at the foot of the South Wall secretly.

牛郎眼睛尖，老早看见了。他假装着没看见，就慢悠悠地四处寻了起来，寻了屋里寻屋外，寻了东院寻西院，待他把天宫寻了个遍，才一步一步寻到南墙根底下，看见那儿正悄悄地趴着只臭虫，老实不客气，伸出两只手指头就把臭虫给捏住了："外公外公，是你不是你呀？不是你我可就要一指头掐碎了。喔，好臭呀！"

Niulang had got good eyesight. He had seen all of that out of the corners of his eyes, but he pretended not to have seen it. Slowly he started to search, from inside the house to the outside, from the east courtyard to the west. After he had searched all over the Palace of the Heaven, finally at the foot of the South Gate he saw a bedbug crawling on the ground. He snatched the bedbug with his two fingers and asked, "Grandpa, is that you? If not, I will clutch it to death. Wow, what a bad smell!"

外公憋不住了，连忙喊出声来："是我，是我，千万别掐了！哎哟喂，把我的胡子都快拔光啦。"

The grandpa could not contain himself any more. He cried, "It is me! It is me! Don't clutch! You damn! My beard is almost pulled up."

牛郎一松手，外公就变了回来，一脸尴尬，好不狼狈。牛郎一边帮着外公整理衣衫，一边就问："外公，你不吃我了吧？"

Niulang released his hand, and the grandpa changed himself back in great embarrassment. While Niulang was arranging the clothes for the grandpa, Niulang asked, "Grandpa, do you still want to eat me up?"

“不吃啦，不吃啦，今天好累，不玩了，你先回去吧。”

"No, no more! I am tired today. I don't want to play. You go back home first."

牛郎回到住的地方，高兴得就想唱歌，织女又跟他说了：“你可别高兴得太早，听我二姐说，外公明天还要和你赌输赢呢。这一会呀，他不变臭虫了，他会变成一颗大桃子，藏在我外婆的衣柜里，你就好好地寻吧。记住了吗？”

When Niulang came back home, he was so excited that he wanted to sing songs. But Zhinu said to him, "Don't be happy so early. I was told by my second elder sister that tomorrow Grandpa will have another bet with you. This time, he will not change himself into a bedbug, but a huge peach hidden in the wardrobe of my grandma instead. Seek him. Clear?"

“记住了，记住了。”牛郎这回有经验了，水来土掩，兵来将挡，嘿嘿，我总有办法对付你的，不怕。

"I see, I see." Niulang said. Now he was very experienced and clever in dealing with this kind of situation. He was not afraid of it any more.

第二天一早，外公又找上门来啦。“外孙女婿，今天咱俩再接着做游戏，我藏你寻。老规矩，寻见了，我免你无罪；寻不见，我还是要吃你。你敢不敢玩？”

The next day, early in the morning, the grandpa came to his house again and said, “Grandson-in-law, let’s play another game today. I hide and you seek. The same rule. If you can find me, I will pardon you; if you can’t find me, I will eat you up. Do you dare to play?”

“外公要我玩，我有啥办法？玩就玩吧。”

Niulang replied, “If Grandpa wants me to play, how dare I say ‘No’? Let’s play it.”

“你先把眼睛闭上，我藏好了就喊你。”

“Close your eyes. Wait until I call you.” the grandpa demanded.

牛郎刚把眼睛闭上，外公“嗖”的一下就变成了一个大桃子，闷声不响躲进了外婆的衣柜。

As soon as Niulang closed his eyes, the grandpa changed into a huge peach instantly, and silently he hid himself in the wardrobe of the grandma.

牛郎还是只当没看见，慢悠悠地就四处寻了起来，寻了屋里寻屋外，寻了东院寻西院，待他把天宫寻了个遍，这才一步一步挨到外婆房里，打开衣柜，看见那块蓝花花的包袱布上静静地躺着一个大桃子，老实不客气，一把拿了过来："外公外公，是你不是你呀，不是你我可就一口吃啦。喔，真香！"

Niulang pretended that he did not know anything. Slowly he began to search, from the inside of the house to the outside, from the east courtyard to the west, until he had searched thoroughly every corner of the Palace of Heaven. Then step by step he moved into the room of the grandma, opened the door of the wardrobe. He then saw a huge peach lying on the bag cloth with the blue dots. He did not hesitate and snatched it and asked, "Grandpa, Grandpa, is that you? If not, I will eat it up. Wow! How sweet the smell!"

外公连忙喊出声来："是我，是我，快放手吧！哎哟喂，我的胳膊都快给你拧断了。"

Hurriedly the grandpa replied, "It is me! It is me! Release your hand! Oh, Damn it! My arms are almost broken."

牛郎一松手，外公连忙又变了回来，一张脸吓得煞白煞白。牛郎还是一副老实巴交的模样，慢悠悠地问着："外公，你不吃我了吧？"

Niulang released his hand. Soon the grandpa changed himself back, pale-faced. Niulang was cautious and prudent but he said slowly, "Grandpa, do you still want to eat me up?"

"不吃啦，不吃啦，今天不玩了，你先回去吧。"

"No, no more. No play today. Go back home first," the grandpa said.

牛郎回到住的地方，织女又跟他说了："一不过二，二不过三。外公哪里肯服输？他明天还要跟你赌输赢呢。他要你藏起来，让他来寻。"

The moment when Niulang came back home, Zhinu told him again, " Things don't stop here. Grandpa will never give in. I was told that tomorrow he will play another game with you. He will ask you to hide and he will seek."

牛郎又为难起来："我这么大个人，藏哪儿去？我又不会变。"

Niulang was very troubled and asked his wife, "where can such a big person like me hide? By the way, I can't change."

织女说："不怕，还有我呢。我来教你变。"

Zhinu said. "Don't be afraid. You still have me. I will teach you how to change."

这天一早，外公又上门了。"外孙女婿，今天咱俩换个花样玩玩，你藏了我寻。要是我寻不见你，我免你无罪；要是被我寻见了，嘿嘿，还是老规矩，我要吃了你。你敢不敢玩？”

The early morning of the next day, the grandpa came to their house again and said, “grandson-in-law, today let’s change our play rule. You hide and I seek. If I can’t find you, you will be pardoned; if I can find you, then the old rule, I will eat you up. Do you dare to play?”

“敢，敢。不就是个死吗？陪你玩一回。你先把眼睛闭上。”

“I dare, I dare, I don’t afraid to die. Let me play with you. Close your eyes.”

外公刚把眼睛闭上，牛郎蹲到地下打了个滚，刹那间变成了一根细细的绣花针。织女眼睛尖，“嗖”的一下捡了起来，就拿着去绣花了。

As soon as the grandpa closed his eyes, Niulang crouched on the ground and had a rolling. Instantly he changed into a slim needle for broidery. Zhinu saw it, and picked it up quickly and with it she started to broider.

织女笑眯眯地说：“外公，外公，牛郎藏起来了，你来寻吧。”

Zhinu said with a smile, “Grandpa, Grandpa. Niulang has hidden himself up. Will you come to seek him?”

外公睁大了眼睛寻，寻了屋里寻屋外，寻了东院寻西院，他把天宫里里外外、上上下下全寻了个遍，却就是寻不见牛郎，他什么事情都想到了，就是没想到自己的外孙女在跟他作对，只好窝着一肚子火回去了。

The grandpa opened his eyes and started to seek, from inside the house to the outside, from the bottom to the top. He searched thoroughly, but in vain. He could have never expected that his own granddaughter was fighting against him together with her husband. He had to leave angrily.

外公前脚刚走，织女后脚就把绣花针朝地上一甩，牛郎“腾”地一下，又站了起来。

Shortly after the grandpa left, Zhinu threw the needle onto the ground and suddenly Niulang stood up.

织女说：“你先别高兴，难的还在后头呢。明天，我外公还要跟你比赛跑步，你在前面跑，他在后面撵。”

Zhinu said, “Keep your guard! The greatest challenge lies ahead. Tomorrow my Grandpa would like to have a running race with you. You run in front, he will chase after you.”

“他能撵得上我吗？”

“Could he catch up with me?” Niulang said.

“怎么撵不上？他跑得可比你快多了。”

“Why not? He runs much faster than you.”

“那怎么办？”

“有办法，有办法。明天比赛的时候，你就挑上一副担子，到我外公的仓库里去畚上满满一箩筐的谷种，再到我外婆的厨房里去拿上满满一箩筐的筷子，都挑上肩。等明天开始比赛，你就照我教你的办法去做，一边跑，一边往地上撒谷种，撒完了谷种再撒筷子。你千万要记住了，要一点一点撒，可别撒多了，越撒得少越好，明白了吗？”

“Then what can I do?”

“I have an idea! When the race begins tomorrow, you carry a burden with you. Before that, you come to my Grandpa’s barn and have a full basket of seed-corns, then come to my grandma’s kitchen and have a full basket of chopsticks. Do as I tell you now. When the race begins tomorrow, you throw the seed-corns first, then the chopsticks. Remember: throw little by little, the less the better. Clear?”

“明白了，明白了，不就是往地上撒谷种吗，撒完了谷种撒筷子，越撒得少越好。你就安心等我的好消息吧。”

“Yes, I do. To throw the seed-corns onto the ground, that is easy, then the chopsticks. The less,the better. Wait for my good news.”

第二天一早，外公又兴冲冲地来叫了："外孙女婿，咱俩再来玩游戏吧。"

The next day, the early morning, the grandpa came happily and said, "Grandson-in-law, let's play another game."

牛郎一脸憨笑："外公外公，你都连输三回了，你还好意思跟我玩游戏吗？"

Niulang smiled naively, and replied, "Grandpa, you have lost the games three times. Do you still want to play with me?"

"好意思，好意思。前三回都是捉迷藏，不稀奇。今天我们动真格的，比赛跑步，你在前面跑，我在后面撵。撵不上，我免你无罪；撵上了，我可还是那句老话，我是非吃你不可的。你敢不敢？"

"Yes, yes! The first three times are hide-and-seek. It is nothing special. But this time I will play serious. Today we are going to have a running race. You run in front, and I will chase after you. If I can't catch you, I will pardon you; if I can, then the old rule. I will have to eat you up. Do you dare to play?"

"不就是撒开腿使劲跑吗？行！我能跑，你先让我准备准备去。"

"Running with the feet? No problem! I can run! But will you please let me do some preparations?" Niulang said.

牛郎回到屋里，找出他上天时用过的那根黄杨木扁担和两只箩筐，到外公的仓库里畚了满满一箩筐谷种，到外婆的厨房里装上满满一箩筐筷子，再披上老牛的皮，一切都准备好了，就跟外公打了声招呼，撒开腿跑了起来。

Coming back home, Niulang took out the boxwood shoulder pole and the two baskets that were used while he was on his way to the Heaven, and went to the barn of the grandpa to take out a full basket of seed-corns, then to grandma's kitchen to load the other basket with the chopsticks. Finally he put on the hide of the ox. When everything was ready, he signaled the grandpa to start.

牛郎在前面跑，外公在后头追。王母娘娘、织女和两个小孩也在后头跟着跑，他们也着急呀，生怕牛郎跑不过他外公，要吃亏。

Niulang was in front running, and the grandfather was chasing after him. Empress Wang, Zhinu and the two kids were running after them. They were worried too, fearing that Niulang would lose to the grandpa and be punished.

牛郎年轻力壮，又披上了老牛的皮，跑起来就像一阵风，好快好快。不过外公更厉害，要知道外公是玉皇大帝，他能坐到这个位置上这么多年，没有点真本事哪能成？没过几个时辰，眼看就要追上牛郎了。牛郎一看，外公要追上来了，猛地想起织女嘱咐过的话，就往地上撒几颗谷种，再过一会儿，又往地上扔一双筷子。扔了筷子再撒谷种，撒了谷种再扔筷子，隔三差五地就这么扔着撒着，撒着扔着。

Niulang was young and strong. With the hide of the ox, he ran as fast as the wind. But the grandpa was even faster. You know, he was the Emperor! If it were not his talents, how could he sustain his position as Emperor? Several hours later, it seemed that he was going to catch up with Niulang. When Niulang looked back and saw that the grandpa was near, it suddenly occurred to him that he might use the tricks that Zhinu had told him before. He started to throw the seed-corns onto the ground, after some intervals, he threw a pair of chopsticks. The chopsticks, then the seed-corns, the seed-corns then the chopsticks, he threw them in turn.

嘿，这一招还真管用呢。牛郎往地下扔什么，他外公就赶紧蹲下来捡什么。撒谷种，他捡谷种；扔筷子，他捡筷子。一样东西也不能白白浪费。一边捡，一边还在嘴里嘟嘟囔囔地唠叨着："看这个外孙女婿，真是个败家子，死到临头了还要糟蹋我家里的东西！"

Wow! This trick did work! Whatever Niulang threw onto

the ground, his grandpa would stoop and pick them up. If they were seed-corns, he picked the seed-corns up; if they were chopsticks, he picked them up too. He did not want to waste even a little bit. As he was picking them up, he did not stop grumbling in his mouth, "Look at you ! The black sheep! You are still wasting the things in my home even before your death."

牛郎一看，怎么他还捡得挺快的，一会儿工夫就又赶上来了，怎么办？他心里一急，就想出了一个办法。他原先撒谷种是几颗一撒，几颗一撒，后来改为一大把一撒，一大把一撒；他原先扔筷子是一双一扔，一双一扔，后来也改为一大把一扔，一大把一扔。他以为这样一来，外公要蹲下去多捡一些工夫，他就追不上来了，谁知道牛郎还是犯了个错误，他偏偏忘记了织女的嘱咐。织女明明说过，要他撒得越少越好，就是为了拖延时间，让外公累得受不了。现在他忘记了这一点，箩筐里的东西很快就少了下去，等到后来，两只箩筐全都空了，没有东西可以撒了，可外公的力气却还没用完，他眼看着就要追上牛郎了。

Niulang looked back. The grandpa was very fast in picking and running. Now he was almost catching up. What to do then? In haste, another idea occurred to him. At the beginning he threw the seeds just by grains, now he changed it by holds. At the beginning he threw the chopsticks by pairs, now he changed it by holds, one hold after another. He thought it might take more time for the grandpa to pick them up that he would never catch up. But he had forgotten what Zhinu had told him before, “The less the better”, in order to prolong the time needed and to exhaust the grandpa. Now he forgot all about it. The things left in the baskets were becoming less and less. And later on, the two baskets were empty, with nothing to be thrown. However, the grandpa had not used up all his energy. On the contrary, it seemed that he was going to catch up with Niulang.

这可怎么办呢?

What to do then?

就在这个千钧一发的紧要关头，王母娘娘出场了。她一时性急，拔出插在自己头上的那支金簪，不管三七二十一，就在玉皇大帝和牛郎之间划了一条线。

Just at this critical moment, Empress Wang appeared. In haste, she pulled out her gold hairpin from her head and made a stroke between Niulang and Jade Emperor.

这一划，可不得了，天上顿时出现了一条波涛汹涌的大河，把玉皇大帝和牛郎给分开了。玉皇大帝过不了这条大河，他也就永远追不上牛郎，当然也就没法再去害死牛郎了。

Do you know what happened then? Suddenly there

appeared a billowy river in the Heaven, which separated Jade Emperor and Niulang. Jade Emperor could not cross the river. He would never catch up with Niulang. Of course, he would never prosecute Niulang any more.

不过，这样一来，王母娘娘同时也犯下了一个天大的错误。这样宽阔的一条大河，不是把牛郎和织女他们一家人也给分开了吗？

However, Empress Wang had also made a great mistake! With the broad river, Niulang and his family had been separated as well.

唉！这就叫越忙越打岔，王母娘娘这个人也真是的，这不是好心帮倒忙吗？你看，你把他们一对恩爱夫妻活活拆散了，作孽呵！

Alas! That is, "Haste makes waste!" What a person Empress Wang was! Was it true that she spoiled all that with her good intention? Look! She had separated the happy couple unintentionally! What a sin!

五、鹊桥相会

5. Meeting at the Magpie Bridge

玉皇大帝要害死牛郎这个外孙女婿，拆散牛郎和织女这一对恩爱夫妻，他是煞费苦心，动足了脑筋。前面三次，他和牛郎捉迷藏，因为织女在边上帮忙，牛郎都赢了。第四次，他和牛郎比赛跑，牛郎一时心慌意乱，把织女嘱咐他的话给忘记了，差一点就要被玉皇大帝追上。就在这个节骨眼上，王母娘娘出来帮忙，拿起金簪这么一划，天上就出现了一条大河，这就是我们今天都能够看得见的天河。

It had been long that Jade Emperor plotted to kill Niulang, the grandson-in-law . For this he had cracked his brains for a long time. For the first three times, because Zhinu was helping Niulang, Niulang escaped. For the fourth time, he wanted to race with Niulang. Out of his nervousness, Niulang had forgotten all that Zhinu had told him in advance, and he was nearly caught up by Jade Emperor. Just at this critical moment, Empress Wang came out to help. She took out her gold hairpin, and drew a river in the sky. That is what we may still see today in the sky, the Milky Way.

不过王母娘娘这个忙还是没有帮好。说起来，玉皇大帝跨不过天河，牛郎的性命倒是保住了。但是这样一来，织女和她的两个孩子不是也过不去了吗？这可怎么办？

However, the help that Empress Wang offered turned out to be a nuisance! It was true that Jade Emperor could not cross the heavenly river to catch Niulang, so that the life of Niulang was saved. But ever since, Zhinu and her kids could not cross the river to see Niulang as well. What to do then?

织女和她的两个孩子天天在天河这边哭着喊着，牛郎天天在天河那边喊着哭着，织女的六个姐姐听着也觉得伤心，就一起向玉皇大帝求情。玉皇大帝把这事的责任推在王母娘娘身上，王母娘娘当然不认账了："什么话？要不是你这个老头子要害自己的外孙女婿，我会拔出金簪来的吗？"

They were crying and shouting every day at this shore while Niulang was shouting and crying at the other. The six sisters were also very sad about it. They came together to plead before Jade Emperor. Nevertheless Jade Emperor shook off the responsibility to Empress Wang while Empress Wang did not acknowledge her mistakes, either. She protested it, "What? If it were not you to persecute your own grandson-in-law, would I pull out my gold hairpin?"

"我不管，一人做事一人当，你闯下的祸，你去收拾场子吧。"

"It's none of my business! It is you who bring about

everything and it is your responsibility to clear up the mess." the Emperor insisted.

两个人吵了三天三夜，到头来也没个结果。

The two quarreled for three days and nights, but without any results.

织女的两个孩子还小，却很有志气，他们两人一商量，就天天跑到天河上舀起水来，发誓非要把天河的水舀干不可。王母娘娘知道了这件事，她也坐不住了，怎么办？就又出了个主意，让喜鹊去传旨，说是从今以后，让牛郎织女两人逢七相会吧。

Young as the two kids of Zhinu, they were ambitious. After their careful consideration, they decided to come to the riverside trying to ladle the water from the river, swearing that they would not stop ladling water from the river until the river was dry. Empress Wang was greatly touched by this. She could not sit on any more. Then she thought of an idea. She asked the magpie to send out the message that ever since then, Niulang and Zhinu could be met at the days when there was a seven in each month.

逢七相会，总比不能相会要好得多，扳指头一算，一个月有三个逢七的日子，一年也就有三十六次了。

It was better than never. If you count the dates, you might

see that in every month they may meet at least three times. That is, thirty-six times in a year.

喜鹊一高兴，生怕自己忘记了，就一边飞，一边在嘴里不停地念叨着："七、七、七……"

The magpie was extremely happy that it murmured all the way in case she would forget it, "seven, seven, seven..."

等到喜鹊飞到天河边上宣旨的时候，它一时慌乱，竟说成了"逢七七相会"。

When the magpie arrived at the riverside to declare the decree, she declared in a hurry, "You may meet on every seventh day of the seventh month."

哎哟哟，这可不得了！多了一个"七"，这个日子就大不一样了。一年当中，只有七月初七这一天，才可以叫做"七七"的。这样一来，牛郎织女就只好在每年七月初七这一天相会，一年只相会一次，太少了，太少了！

Oops! What a mistake! Another seven was added to it and what a difference it was! There is only one day in a year that is "the seventh day of the seventh month". That is the origin of the festival "Double Seventh Day"! So Zhinu and Niulang could only meet on the seventh day of the seventh month, once in a year!

王母娘娘的旨意是不能随便改的，传错了就只好将错就错。从此以后，牛郎和织女两人就只好在七月初七这一天渡过天河来相会。

However, the decree of Empress Wang should not be altered at will. Even though it was a mistake, you had better accept it. Ever since then, Niulang and Zhinu could only meet on the seventh day of the seventh month across the heavenly river.

喜鹊犯了这么个大错误，它也难过啊！大家都骂它，说它不会办事，把牛郎织女这对夫妻害惨了！喜鹊痛下决心，要将功补过，它就一个劲地生儿孵子，子子孙孙，成千上万，到了每年七月初七这一天，老喜鹊就带着它的后代子孙，一齐到天河边上去。这只喜鹊咬着那只喜鹊的头，那只喜鹊咬着这只喜鹊的尾巴，你咬着我，我咬着你，大伙儿齐心协力，连成了好长好长的一大串，就在天河上临时搭起了一座鹊桥来啦。

Since the magpie had made a mistake, she was very upset too. People started to curse her, saying she was good at nothing but to separate Niulang and Zhinu. The magpie made up her mind to do certain remedies for that. Then she laid more eggs and hatched them out. The sons and grandsons multiplied by thousand. Every year on the seventh day of the seventh month, the old magpie, along with her off-springs, gathered altogether at the riverside, with one magpie biting the tail of the other.

You bit mine and I bit yours, with the joint efforts of the team, they were clustered in a long queue. At the riverside they built a Magpie Bridge!

牛郎和织女踩着喜鹊的头顶，一步一步走过去，在这座鹊桥上相会。他们哭哭讲讲，讲讲哭哭，有着说不完的知心话。喜鹊的身体很小，它们怎么受得了两个大人的重量？所以到了后来，天底下所有喜鹊的头顶上都是光秃秃的不长毛，老人说起来，都说这就是牛郎织女踩出来的。老人们还说，平常日子里，我们到处都可以看见喜鹊在天上飞，就是到了七月初七这一天，看不见喜鹊了，到处都看不见喜鹊了。为啥？原来到了每年的这一天，地上的喜鹊全都飞到天上，替牛郎织女搭桥去啦。这样一来，地上也就看不见喜鹊了。喜鹊怕这件事让玉皇大帝知道了要受到处罚，所以总是快去快回，七月初七傍晚飞上天，第二天天不亮就又赶紧飞回到地上来，年年都是这样。时间一长，大伙儿都原谅喜鹊了，都说它的好话。俗话说："喜鹊叫，喜事到。"据说也是这么来的。

Niulang and Zhinu stepped on the heads of the magpies, step by step they moved on to meet on the Magpie Bridge. They cried and talked and talked. It seemed that they always had a lot to talk with each other. The bodies of the magpies were tiny. How could they sustain the weights of the two adults? So later on, the heads of the magpies became bald. Elders say that it was because of the trampling of Niulang

and Zhinu. The elders also say that at other times there were a lot of magpies flying here and there, but when that day came, all of the magpies disappeared suddenly. Why? They had all gone to the Heaven to help build the Bridge. That is why few magpies could be seen on the Earth that day. The magpies were afraid of the Emperor's knowledge of that, so they always flew in a hurry. At the dusk of the seventh day of the seventh month, they flew to the sky. At the dawn, they flew back. Every year it was like this. With the passage of time, people began to forgive the magpies, and spoke highly of their loyalty. Here comes another ancient saying, "Magpie arrives, good thing happens." Perhaps it is also out of this very reason.

世世代代传下来，大家把七月初七的晚上叫做“七夕”，人人都要过这个节日。到了夜深人静的时候，年轻人躲在葡萄架底下，兴许还能偷听到牛郎和织女两个人说的悄悄话呢。

From generations to generations, this story was passed down. Now, that special day is also called *"Double Seventh Day" (QiXi)*. When that day comes, people celebrate it. Late at night when everything is silent and quiet, young people will come to the grape canopies to overhear the whispers of Niulang and Zhinu.

据说，织女老是在埋怨牛郎：“我嘱咐你要撒得越少越好，越少越好，你怎么就忘记了呢？”

It is said that Zhinu always said to Niulang reproachfully, “I have told you to throw the less the better. The less the better, how can you forget them all?”

“嗨，”牛郎也总是后悔得不得了，“可不是吗？我看看外公快追上我了，心里一慌，就把你的话给忘啦。”

“Sorry”, Niulang confessed, “It’s my fault. I saw Grandpa coming near me. I was so nervous that I forgot all that you have told me.”

世世代代传下来，大伙儿都把织女说成是个纺织能手，她心灵手巧，织出来的绢就像天上的云彩那样漂亮。到了这一天晚上，年轻的女孩子们都会聚在一起，在院子里摆上一些供品：瓜呀，菱呀，藕呀，莲蓬呀，花呀，果呀，据说全是织女平日里最爱吃的东西，然后点上香烛，虔诚祭祀牛郎和织女。

Generations by generations, people all say that Zhinu was really a good Zhinu. She was so skillful. The silk she had woven was just like the colorful and beautiful clouds. When that day comes, young girls would like to gather together and put on the tables some offerings such as watermelon, water chestnuts, lotus root, lotus seeds, flowers, nuts and other delicacies. It is said that these are all the favorite foods of Zhinu. Then candles are lit and Niulang and Zhinu are

worshiped piously.

这时候，她们还要向织女“乞巧”。乞巧的风俗，各个地方都不太一样。有的地方，女孩子们会取来雨水和井水各一半，盛在一只碗里，在露天里先放上一夜，再放在太阳底下晒上半天，到了中午，水面上就会有一层薄薄的水膜。这时候，再拿来一枚绣花针，轻轻巧巧地放下去，让它浮在这层水膜上面。这时候，大家凑在一起，兴致勃勃地去看那枚针在水中究竟映出一种什么样的影子来。这种影子总是很有趣的，如果像龙凤，像云彩，像花朵儿，大家就会非常高兴，说这是个好兆头，预兆着这个女孩子将来一定会心灵手巧，事事如意，还能找个如意郎君呢。这就是“乞巧”。因为常常是许多女孩子聚在一起“乞巧”，所以大伙儿又叫它“乞巧会”。

At this time, they usually pray for ingenuity from Zhinu. This custom differs from place to place. In some areas, the girls would like to gather half bowl of rainwater and half bowl of well-water. Then they mix them together in one bowl. The bowl has to be put outside the house overnight, then to be exposed in the sun for half a day. When midday comes, a thin layer of water membrane will be found on the surface of the water. At that time, they would like to take out a needle for embroidery, cautiously put it down onto the water membrane. People usually gather together to watch the reflection out of the needle from the surface of the water. The reflection is very interesting. If it is like the images of the dragon and the phoenix, or the clouds, or the flower buds, people would be very happy, saying this is a good sign. This shows that the girl will be very skillful, and be smooth in everything, and can marry a good husband. That is "to pray for ingenuity". Since it is a custom for the girls to gather together to pray for ingenuity from Zhinu, the meeting is usually called "*Praying Meeting*".

在"乞巧会"上，大伙儿总是要再讲一遍牛郎织女的故事。大概正是因为这样一些原因吧，牛郎织女的故事也就在中华大地上一代一代传下来，一直传到了今天。

On the Praying Meeting, the story of Niulang and Zhinu is usually told one more time. Perhaps it is out of this very reason that this story has been spread out throughout China from generations to generations, until up to now.